Bultman

Moments I Live

Bultman

Bultman717@gmail.com

ISBN: 978-0-578-69966-0 (Paperback)

Library of Congress Control Number: 2020909778

Front cover image by Ivan Bultman
Book design by Ivan Bultman
Interior images by Kendall Leggate
Drawn art by Ivan Bultman

First printing edition 2020

Website:
Bultmanshop.com
Instagram:
@bultman717

Bultman

I dedicate this to YOU

W o r d s l o v e
W o r d s h a t e
W o r d s g i v e

\-

B u l t m a n

table of contents

dear creator.
can you hear me?
why do i feel this way?
why am i here?
i dont know who i am or who i will become
but my story is of pain.
my heart may be filled with tears but i
have the desire to love.
i need you to know that i am just like
anyone.
i am like the people around me. . .
we all have our own chapter of life.
this one is mine.

Moments I Live

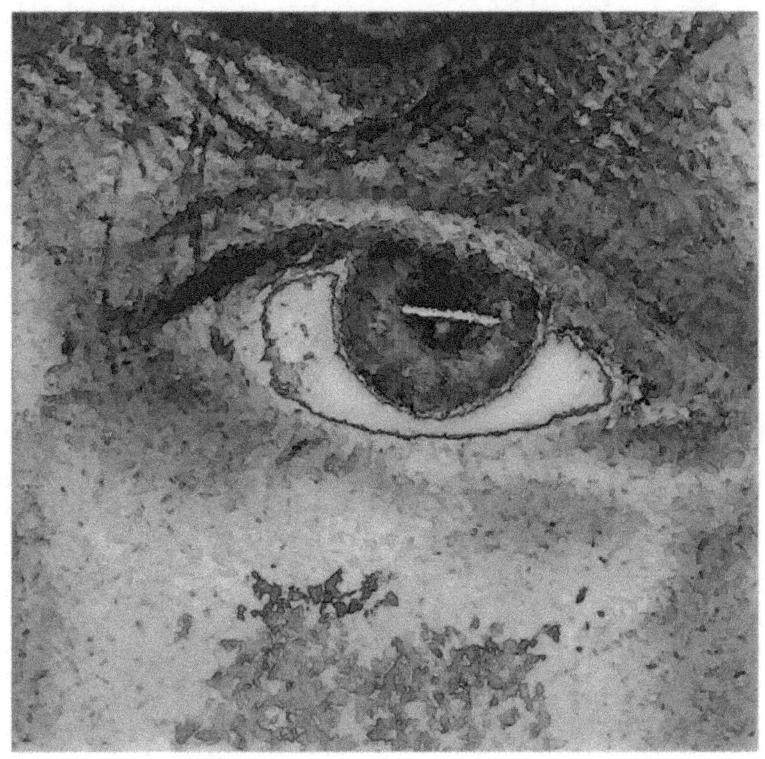

Chapter One
The Beginning

I cried so much the fishbowl became clear again.

Moments I Live

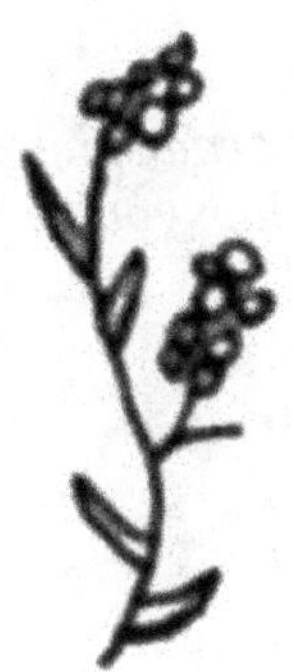

The Cry

The tears
and fears
All have a reason why.
Can I exist within your atmosphere?
That I still hold onto when you're here?
Can I... can I...?
This is my cry for help.
The cry for you, Dear friend.

This all has a reason why.
I hope it's not goodbye
When it's too late to say hi,
because this is my cry.
The cry for help.

This has a reason for change.
The cry for help...
I guess this is goodbye then....
I never got to say that.....
and I never told you.....
so why don't you tell me?
Why don't you let my feelings go?

This was my cry for help,
To cry the years away,
To cry before the rainbow...

This is the last goodbye.
I'm glad I never said hi to you...
It would hurt too much to do.
I can't say goodbye
but I won't let you
hold me down.
This was my cry for help.
The Cry was for you my, Dear friend.

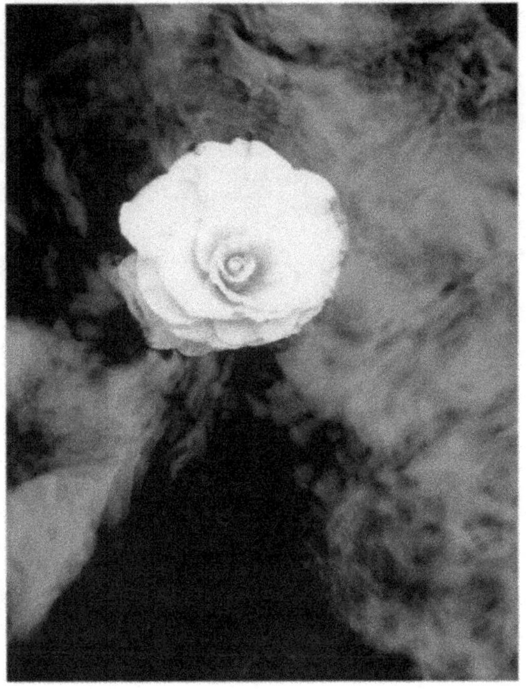

Perfectly souled

If you cry a little at night,
Die a little inside.
Then you're perfectly souled to me. . .

Lovin' You

When it hurts,
When it burns,
Tell me only your truth.
Tell me all the wrongs you made.
Tell me you hate me
because that would be the truth.
I've been waiting for the honesty
to shine through in your heart.

How crazy you made me feel
for believing in the lies.
I fell in love with a broken person
and I still need help to let go of you.
You're not my perfect soul anymore;
and I'm not your best friend
that will come and save you.
I'm not your only love...
anymore.
but I'm so used to lovin' you.
When it hurts,
When it burns,
When you hate on me,
When you lied to me...
I loved every bit of your truth.

Leave Me Alone

I would rather be
in deep sleep than with you.
Just leave me alone.
I have bones
that broke by your ways and white lies.
You have a wall
that I would rather jump off of
then climb over to be with you.
So please, just leave me alone.

?

What makes you want to stay?

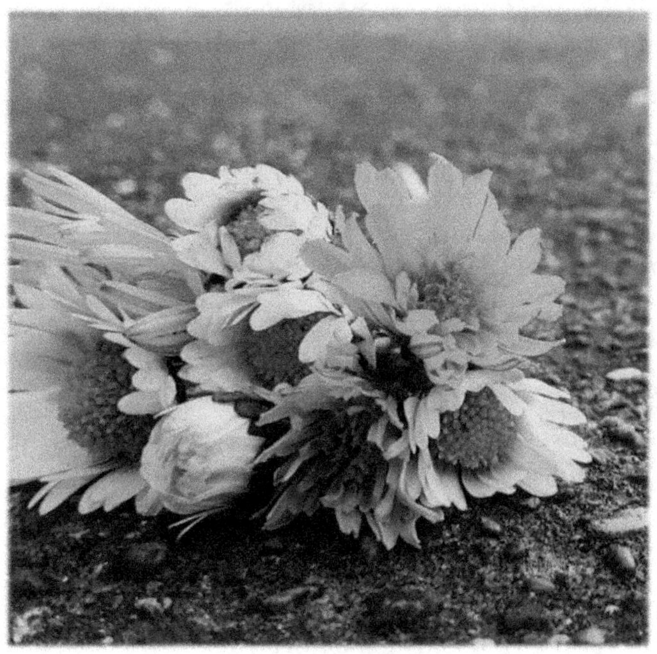

Before I Go

Before I go,
Tell me you're never letting go.
Before I jump,
Tell me you'll hold my hand.
Let me know
if you need some space.
I need to know if I'm wrong.
Before I go, please give me your hand.
I might never see your glowing eyes again.
I know you all too well
but it's hard to say it now.

Before I go to that avenue,
Let me know your thoughts, please.
Tell me to stay,
but before I go, I want to say
I have never really felt this way.
I fell from a dream in the summer.
I fell again back in November.
I tripped over the way you held me,
The way you felt...
I never really lost myself before you.

I knew what I wanted, and that was goodbye,
because I never knew
that you were cold in your veins.
Now I know who you were.
Now I know what you wanted.
All I know is what I want now:
for you to know I still care about you
and I will be fine without your bad weather
but before I go,
I must say
I am not around,
so please don't knock.

In the Dark

"Can you crawl out of a dark space?
because just know I can't.
Do you know what's in there?
Where my shadows lived?
Where I disappeared for a while?
It's that dark space.
Our dark space"

.

Who are you?
Where are you?
I can't see you.
Are you standing over there?
Are you in the dark?
Will you come out and play?
I don't like these games.
Don't list off all their names.
I can't stand this noise.
Are you in the dark?
Why won't you come out?
Is it where I lay my head?
I hear voices in my head.
Can I see your face?
I wanna know
Who you are,
Where you are.
Are you standing there?
I will fall into the dark,
to find you.

Run to You

I dream of you at night.
You're made of pure moonlight.
This is something I couldn't fight.
I knew you were always right.
I should run to you.
We cant fly away...
but I don't want to stay on the ground.
I don't want you to float away
Like a lost balloon.
When I get to you,
I will run to you.
You will be safe in my arms.
This love is painted violet
like the night sky.
I was going to run to you;
but I only dreamt of this.
This is only a minor fantasy.
I can't wait to run to you,
because you're just a true love. . .
I never had.

Construction Trucks

You bring me up
and smash me down.
I used to think I required you,
when I didn't understand myself.
I guess I fell in love.
Don't say I just quit you,
all I ever did was tell you everything.
Now I regret our love.
I can't believe you broke my truck,
and never fixed me up.
You took a big wrecking ball,
and smashed through my every window.
and all I ever expected...
was for you to fix me.
All you ever did to me was,
break me and my mirrors
and crash into me like burning bumper cars.
I guess I fell under a spell,
and never questioned why,
because all you ever did was crash my construction truck.

All you ever did was hit me up,
when you wanted me to save you.
Never did you really love me,
and now you really build to the sky,
but it seems it may fall one day.
Don't you ever say I just left you there.
You made a mistake here.
I didn't break your construction truck;
All I did was build you up.
and now I am out of air.
Can't breathe up here,
and now I am crashing down.
Wait to hear me shatter.
because all you ever did was build me up
and tear me down,
and I never once saw you frown.
You said we were never really good,
and now you made our skyscraper fall.
I never knew anything at all about you.
All I know now is the cold ground.
I am broken up,
I will never truly be found again.
so build your skyscrapers up so high,
Like all the lies you held in your front yard.
as I acted surprised by each one.
Never did I break you down,
or crash your trucks.
Your construction truck has always been untouched.

Respect it

Wish it,
so that I can be in your dreams one day.
Know it,
so we don't cross any lines.
Give it,
so I am not the only one showing love.
Say it,
so that I feel your passion.
Bless it,
so we can be better soon.
Respect it,
so that I don't get my feelings hurt.

You need to learn to love.
I can't believe us right now.
You don't get it, still.
Why don't we have kind words?
Respect it;
You will get it.
You always knew it.
Listen to me now,
When I say something,
Don't judge me.
This isn't fun anymore,
so get the message.
so you respect it,
because we will get better soon.

Chapter Two
My... My... Feelings

My Heart
My Regrets
The Chairs Are Empty
Interlude . Mixtape
Bunny Oh' Worries Gone
My Lost soul
Clouded Emotion

How can you feel good about this?

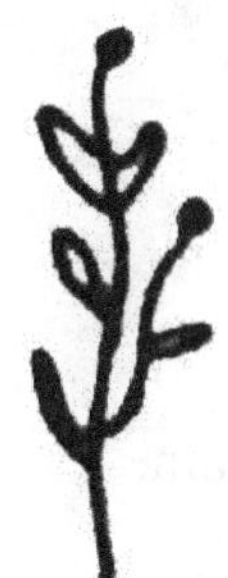

My Heart

Fragile.
I can't believe it fell in two.
I'm on my way,
but my heart...
It needs time,
It takes time away.
It wants you, and it doesn't.
My heart
has been hurt before,
and wants to be hurt again.
My heart
needs love.
It wants to be alone.
It is indecisive.
It is loving.
My heart...
All it wants is to beat next to you sometimes.

My Regrets

I have regrets.
I lost twice.
I have regrets in my head.
I have them beneath my toes.
I never know if it's wrong or right.
I have regrets,
I can't lie about that.
I can't be nice with this in my head.
I want to be good.
What is good for you?
Why can't I sleep at night?
My crazy life is catching up.
My regrets are filling my head.
My life is full of regrets.
No, No my head is filled with regrets.
Have I ever done something for me?
Have I been the best?
My regrets. . .
I have way too many.
Yes, I have regrets,
but *who doesn't?*

The Chairs Are Empty

Let me sing a song...
If I could have held your hand,
I would have done it by now.
If we could be friends,
I would have stopped right now,
but all I see are empty faces in the room,
and I don't see you.

The chairs are empty.
someone help me.
I think I am going crazy,
and I think I lost my mind.
I would walk across a river
for a friend like him.
I would have jumped across any ocean to find you.

The chairs are now emptied out,
and nobody cares
to come and say their prayers.
If I could run to him,
I would tell him,
"Don't do it, please,"
because I need you here,
I really do.

Now the chairs are abandoned.
They sit in a circle,
Nobody sitting there but me.
The chairs are empty still.

If I could have seen you. . .
I would have been near you then,
To see you before the accident.
Now, nobody cares
That the chairs
Are empty.

I can breathe now,
I feel his happiness above.
Nobody told me I would feel lonely,
but I am.
. . . I could have been there,
but I wasn't,
and now the chairs around me,
The ones that surround me,
The one he used to sit in,
The place we used to be in
Together,
Is empty now.

Interlude .
Mixtape

Treated Right is Sustainable, Tell A Nobody.

I play it all the time.
From A to B, it's pretty crazy.
I hear your voice on the mixtape.
Hope you feel better soon.
That mistake put me in fear,
Then I knew what really happened.

Bunny Oh' Worries Gone

Tears fall down my face;
Holding onto bunny so I don't suffocate.
I guess I wasn't good enough
to be her favorite?
So howl at the top of your lungs because
even the ones who care can't hear me cry now.
They say to call the Doctor,
Get some sleep,
but all that ever did for me was.....
Shove medication down my throat.
Tell me Bunny Oh' worries gone . . .

My Lost soul

Is it completely gone?
I don't know.
Is love still here?
No one cares.
My soul was taken.
My soul is gone.
but why, I still cry,
is it gone?
Do I still love?
Was it taken?
or is it still here?
Do I cry for him?
My lost soul loves,
My lost soul cares,
My lost soul was taken,
My lost soul cries,
My lost soul tells lies.
My lost soul was always mine.
My lost soul is here with me now.

Clouded Emotion

Don't jump to conclusions;
This is normal.
I have clouded emotions.
I can't feel like an ocean.
I want to be independent,
but I'm not.
I have clouded emotion,
Need to put the feelings away.
My unhinged life can't take it anymore.
My life is unstable,
but this is my reality.
My unstable life.
I have to put up my feelings.
I feel the ocean now.
I feel normal.
With all this leftover emptiness,
This is clouded emotion
. . .it stays in my being,
Day and night.
My unstable life holds it all,
My clouded emotion ends with no reason.

Chapter Three
Lonely isn't Bad?

If being with others is exhausting, then being alone should be bliss.

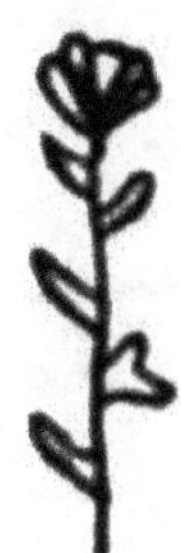

eractnodi

Everything I touch is so silver...
I feel nothing now.
I feel like I lost my heart.
I don't care about the things I use to love.
normal is me now.

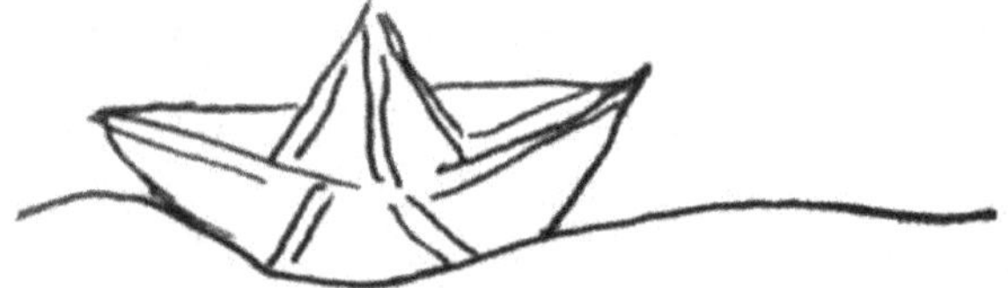

9 sailboats

So many other things painted before you
but now the eyes around us
watching our every move,
When you hold my hand I only see you.
When the waves crash and people break...
Just know I see you
in every form you take
you're painted like a Van Gogh.
You hold a light in every move
your hands calm me
right down from planet nine.
You paint my heart
like a sunset setting in winter.
I hope you can feel me
and my energy on its way
to the light you hold high.
I count your demons
and I show you mine
in broken time.
The waves crash and you form
the light that takes me by storm.
The energy holds my breath
in your hands
and the way you can shake me...
Nothing you do breaks me.

Thanks Again

You wanted a savior,
I was a liar.
Thanks again for telling me,
I couldn't give you everything,
You just wanted a beautiful lie to live.
I couldn't give you the dream,
so you took my light.
I wanted to leave,
You pushed me to stay.
I know I was in the wrong,
You know I tried to make it right.
Thanks again for loving me,
I know I should have focused on us
but thanks again for leaving me.

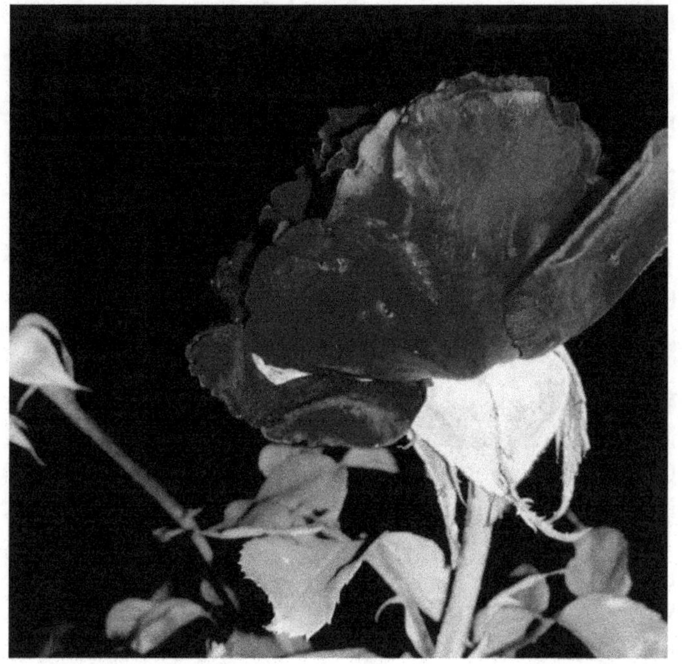

Should Forget

Locked out from the love...
How can I give more to yuh?
I won't erase this from my memory,
Even if yuh leave me in infinity.
Right now I feel betrayed
like the faces of hell
are laughing right at me.
This distance makes yuh give in
but I don't care
if I'm forgotten thoughts.

Yuh keep the key
in that worn-out pocket
that still feels red
like the lights in the room.
The alarms one by one
break into blue
when my heart breaks for you.
I am tired of running
on this path that doesn't
get back to yuh.

My emotions are flickering
like the hallway lights,
Greens and yellows broken between us.
I want yuh to just give in to us
before I become a forgotten thought
once in for all
but I need yuh more than I want to
lose the memory.
So many times I could just forget yuh.....
but *who would want to?*

Nobody Can Help Me

I have been feeling
like people
Just don't get me.
I have a problem,
because nobody
Can help me at all.
Nobody can tell my mind
to shut the hell up;
The thoughts don't ever want to leave.
Even if I walk alone,
The thoughts come around each time.

"You're worthless"
"You will be nothing"
"You're FAKE"

6

You were so selfless to put me first of all the flowers.
I can't wait to float on the boat of the lucky one.

Bleed

5 more minutes,
I lay here to bleed.
One more hour,
and it will all be over.
I can't keep losing myself.
I fight for what I want,
I need to move on,
I need to get up.
I can patch up the cuts.
I know I was a failure,
To him and her.
I know I could have been there,
but I was here bleeding on my own.

You wanted better,
I let you leave me in tears.
5 more minutes,
I lay here to bleed.
Every hour,
I miss you.
One day I will move on,
I loved you and I wanted to go with you.
I know you want me to live,
I just want to see you again.

Bleeding is a part of life,
We all bleed alike.
I try to patch up my cuts,
but they are infected,
From the memories of you.

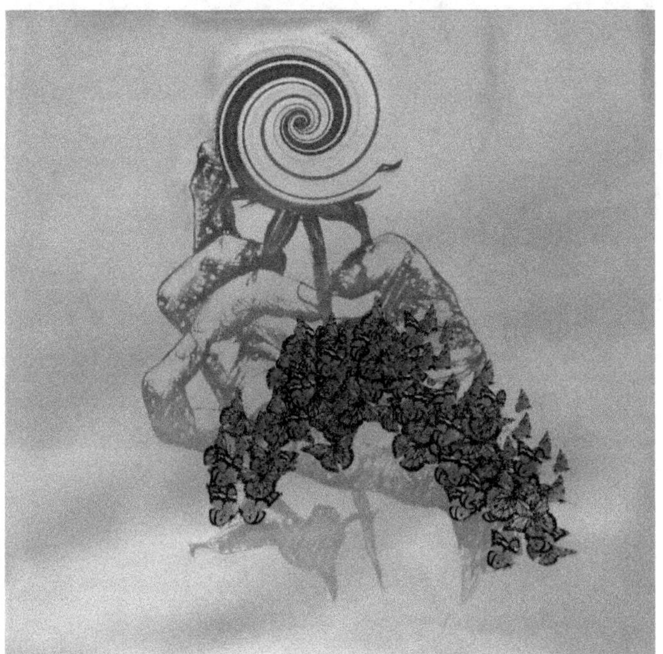

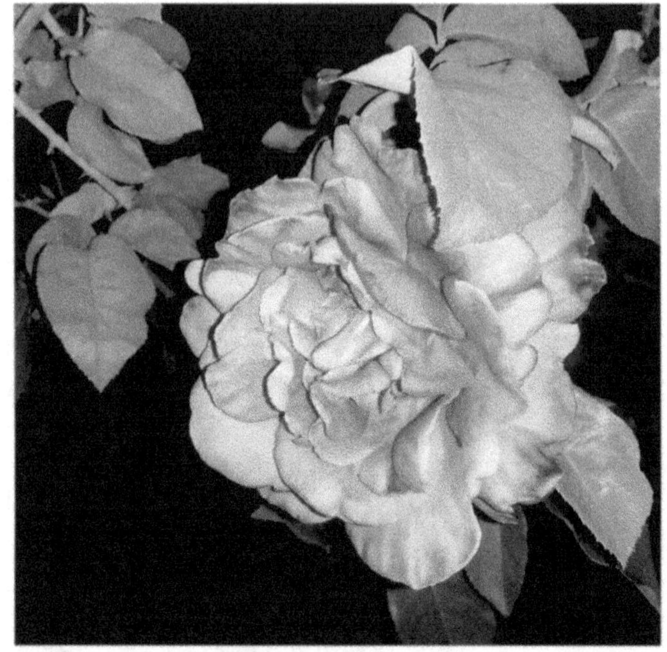

3

You say the cruel words to my face
and at least you're being honest.
I fall like a lightweight from grace.

Cold Corners

Curtains closed,
Darkness spills onto the floor.
Still standing alone in that room,
Feeling the air,
of the broken fan hit my back.
I could have sworn I heard you laugh.
I fell to my cold corners,
When you hurt me.
I didn't see this coming,
You killed,
and I'm now with the wind.

How could you do this to me?
Did I not make you happy?
I seem to hurt a lot,
It's my fault for loving you.
So I'm gonna be right here,
Where the air is cold and there is fear.

I am gonna be okay,
I need you to know.
I would rather give up the breath,
Then love you,
I will be here in my cold corners.
You always said I made great company,
Did you lie to my face?
I said I loved you,
You always doubted me.

Now I doubt you,
and I stick to my room.
Haven't eaten in a week,
Seems my bones have gotten weak.
I am saying goodbye,
for the last time.
My cold corners never felt so warm.

Alone Again

I remember letting that friend go...
You had to say goodbye.
It's so much clearer now.
I know that I was going to fall;
You dropped me off a cliff.
I know it's a mistake that you made.
You didn't have to let me go.
How am I supposed to be alone?
I must stay in the same place as last night.
I think you know that I am alone again.
I won't be calling anymore.
You fell out of my life.
Don't forget, it's over.
I let you go.
I hope you sleep alone.
because I think I am going to be happier
if I am alone again.
You see that this was a mistake.
Your biggest mistake.

Romance is Dead

Romance is dead to me
like the apple trees in the winter.
She didn't kiss me before the
clock ticked out forever
Instead, she smiled
and left in December.
Romance is dead to me
like the bird on the street.
I can't steal the hearts left in the trees because
Romance is done with me.

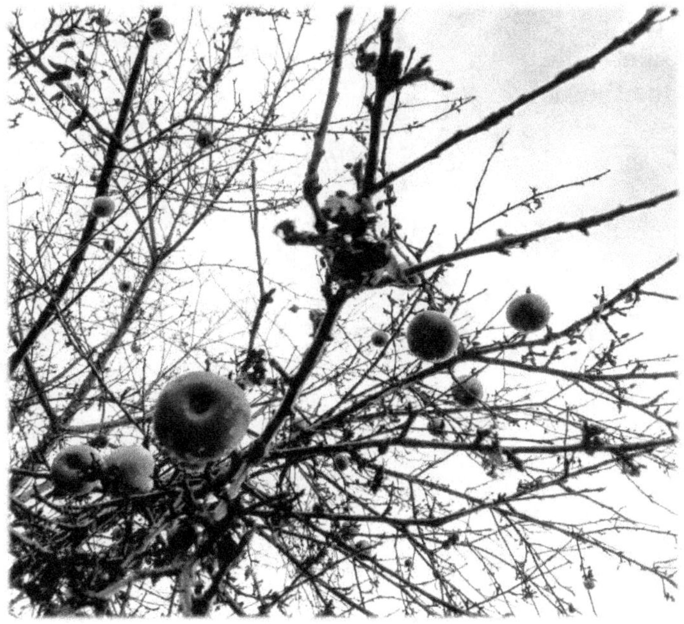

Chapter Four
Day to Day

Live every hour like it's the last you will ever have.

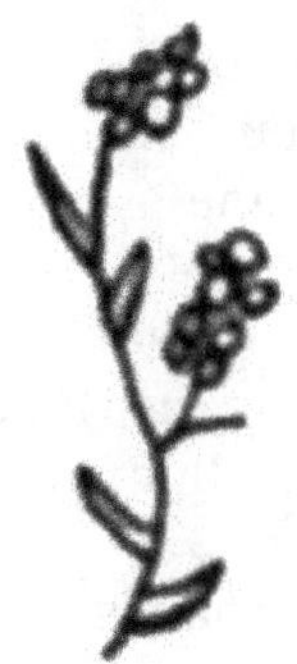

Emotion

I love you.
I cry for you.
I can't stand you. . .
This is my ride with you.
Emotion drives me insane.
That's because of you.

My emotion is always on the run to you,
Never wanting anything but you.
This is more than love;
This is my trust in your hands,
My heart out in the open.

This emotion left me,
When you did.
Now I'm all alone,
I have sealed up my emotions,
My emotion is somewhere out there.

Yuh

Yes Unless Hurting,
You Used His Heart.

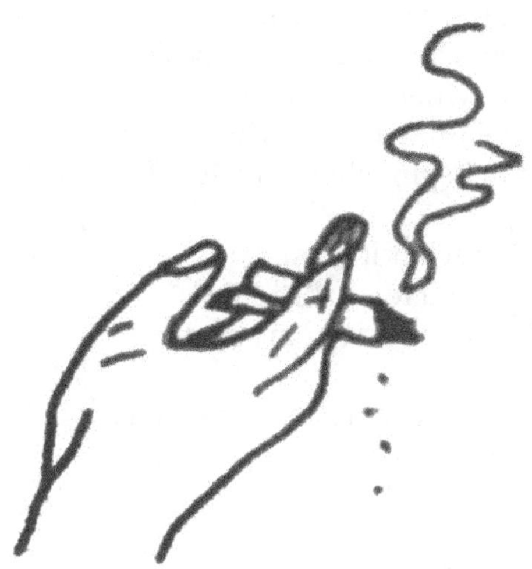

Into the Light

I see stars when I see it,
I see hope when I see it,
I see fear when I see it,
I see fate when I see it.
I see life in my hands when I see it,
I see my past when I look upon it.

I see the dark hiding from it,
I feel free when it touches my skin,
I feel love when I see its beauty,
I feel hopeful when it arrives,
I hear life begin when it thrives.

I would touch it if I could,
I would bleed for it if I could,
I would die for it to come again
... but,
What I love most about it is when I
Step into its light.

Many Moons Ago

Many moons ago,
I made her mine.
The first sight was near...
This was the first of many days we spent.
The night to morning is always a mystery...
but many moons ago I lost her.
I lost myself.

Many moons ago,
I gave someone all of my trust,
so they didn't feel insecure.
I fell for the love,
because I needed it.
This has been a rocket ship flight;
I don't know what's next in life.

Many moons ago,
I gave my heart away.
I made myself a fool.
I turned around
with a knife in my back.
I can't dream of more moons,
but that was many moons ago...

Save Me as A Draft

Just save me as a draft when you're done with me
You don't even have to publish me.
Save me as a draft.
I don't want to be trash……s..a..v..e…..

Told You so

I remember saying that you were wrong,
I knew all along that I was right.
I told you so when I said goodnight.
Now I don't feel life....
I am questioning everything....
Everything I said.
I told you,
I am not good enough for you.

Hurt

I speak of light,
but it wasn't my intention.
My life was colder than any winter storm.
Don't let me absorb the light.
That light took her,
Took him,
Took all of them.
It tore my heart apart.
It hurt me in the ways hell can't.
The light hurts.

Glass

Broken windows,
Broken mirrors,
Broken picture frames.
I cut out the pain.
I cut *you* out
Of every picture.
The glass shows
My shattered heart.
Loving me isn't easy,
but I cut out the pain.
I cut you out because you're hazardous.
if you don't love me, tell me.
I will break the glass between us.

Broken and Bleeding

I almost always give in to the hate.
I know you know I forget things,
I am sorry for everything.
I know that now your heart is broken
but, my body is bleeding without you.

Moments I Live

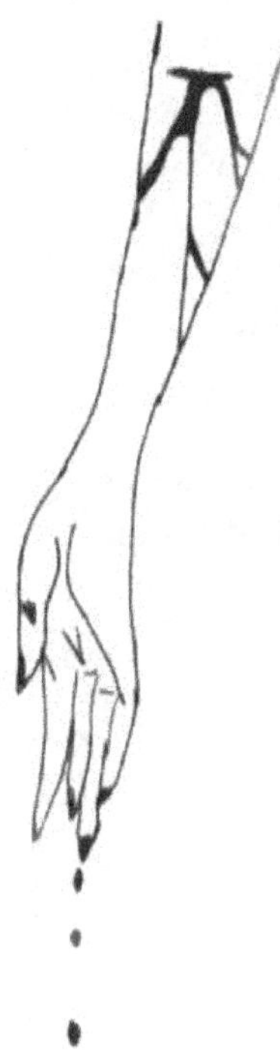

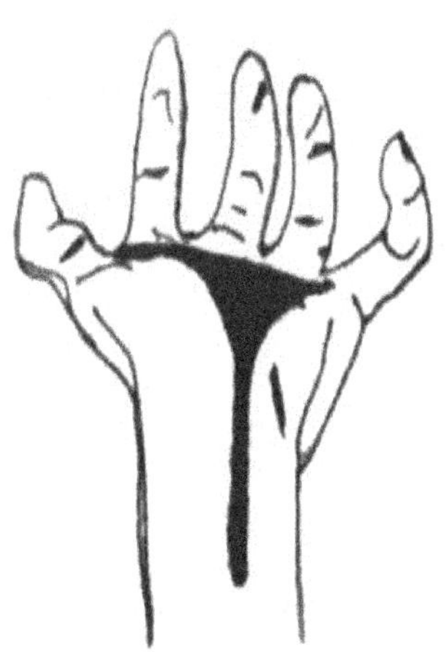

6/14 At Noon

12 P.M.
Scared.
I can't believe it's over...
Silent hallways
The end as I know.
This is the last day
of being this person.
I want to stay,
but visiting hours are over.
Today was 6/14 at noon.

Touch

You got that green eye,
I got that nightlight,
I see you standing in the moonlight.
The fire is burning,
Water flowing,
'Cause you got that
Touch.

Quiet

No motion.
Where is the sound?
There are no words,
it's just quiet.
No noise,
Just quiet.
There is no cry for help,
it's just quiet.
No voice,
Not even mine.
Just quiet.

One Word

One word is all it takes
One word makes or breaks
One word lives on and one doesn't
One word loves,
One word hates,
One word forgives,
One word disappears...
One word can love me,
but one word can change me.

Chapter Five
Running Free

It's time to move on from this stop sign.

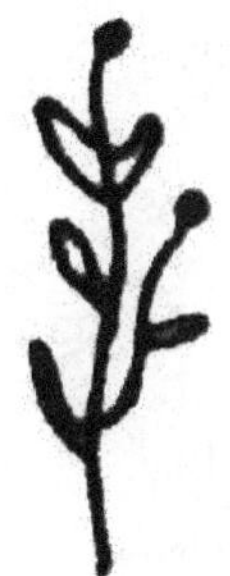

Graduate

When the clock strikes midnight,
We are no longer trapped.
We can't believe it's over.
We did it.
At least most...
We just graduated.
So now we can live how we want to;
Without school rules,
but still with responsibility.
I can't be carefree,
but I get to be me,
so now I'm happier.
I graduated.
I did it by myself.
I get better each day.
I hope we graduate to be better people.

The Run

I run
not for fun
I scream in the light
I hide in the night
It's in plain sight
This doesn't feel right
I can't see what she sees in me
It doesn't matter to me
Can't you see what I see?
I need time for my run
This is not fun
I can't do it
How will I get through it?
Will I push through?
Can I see it better now?
Can I live in the night?
Will I take flight?
Can I see the stars?
I look up to find the night
but I see the light
I can't live like this anymore
This is my run from the cages.

Zig-Zag

Going both ways
Heading left and right
I got caught up in a zig-zag
I can't be doing this right.
I seem to fall behind,
because I keep running in a zig-zag.
I can't keep going one way.
No, no, yes, yes...
I'm going in a zig-zag,
They tell me to stay on my path,
but I just took a left.
I'm not at a stoplight,
Just sitting in the sunlight.
Still going in a zig-zag,
I'm on a good path,
The line going left and right,
Still in a zig-zag.
I can't really get in line,
This zig-zag made me better though.
I'm on this zig-zag forever.

Serious

"Take this seriously."
Why?
"because it's right."
and being different is wrong?
"Just act serious."

They say serious,
but why even bother?
Serious is right,
Serious never causes a crisis,
but it's never real to who I am.
I want to be me,
Not someone I'm not,
Why be anyone but me?

"Take this seriously."
"No."
"Just act serious."
"I'm not going to act for you."
I'm going to be me
and if that's so wrong,
Then be serious and put up with it.

Damaged Goods

Something damaged me,
My question is *what?*
Is it love?
Is it trust?
Is it honesty?
Somebody tell me.
Is it my broken heart?
My love for somebody?
My heart wanting more?
Something damaged me,
but what is it?
Is it you?
Is it me?
Is it the way I disagree?
The way I speak to you?
The way I love you?
Tell me
am I Damaged Goods?
Tell me nobody wants me.
but something hurt me.
My question is what?
Is it my love for you?
or the way I lost you?

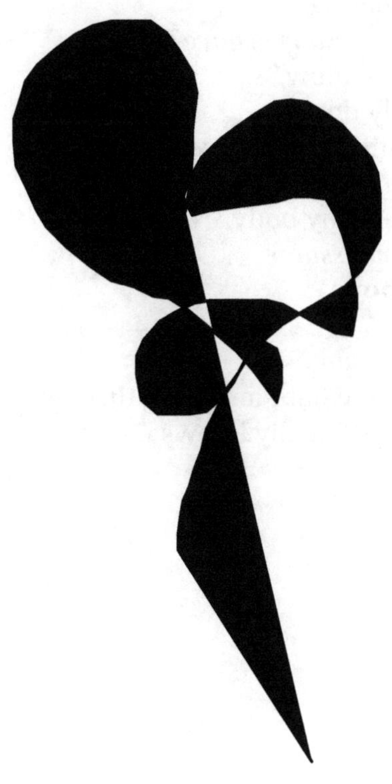

assume

Never good enough.
Why is that an issue we have?
You think you know,
but you really don't.
So stop assuming you know.
You don't have my feelings,
You don't have my body.
So why do you assume?
That I like boys
or girls.
Why do you assume
that you know what I am going through?
because nobody really knows me at all.

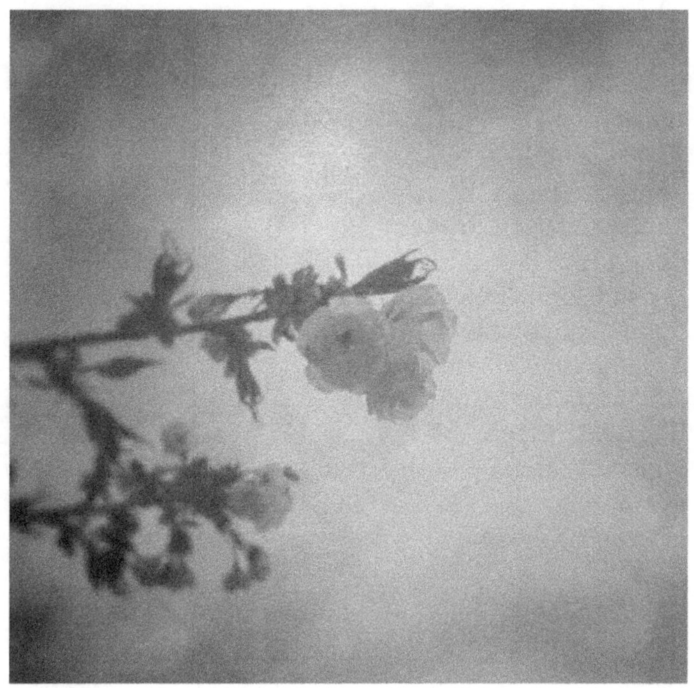

Buy a Heart

Does anyone want to buy,
Purchase this heart for cash,
Trade for love?
What is the point if I don't feel?
it's too much.
There is a heart for sale.
I don't care who trades.
I don't care if you steal.
I wish I could love like you...
but would you buy a heart?
Buy and then give or trade?
Love and then throw it away?
Buy a heart from me.
I need to catch up with actuality.
I want to love,
but can't have love.
I want you,
but I can't have you.
I need love,
but don't have love.
I need you,
but don't have you.

Could you buy a heart?
Purchase it for the low price of free,
Trade for love,
Trade for a heart,
Trade for something more?
What's the point if I don't feel?
it's too much.
There is a heart for sale.
I don't care who buys.
I don't care if you steal.
All I want
All I need
is to be loved,
but this heart doesn't work.
so who is buying my broken heart?

Chapter Six
The Small Kitchen

Lemon
Washed Off On Me
Meat
Glass Half Full
Can't Eat

Watch what you eat.

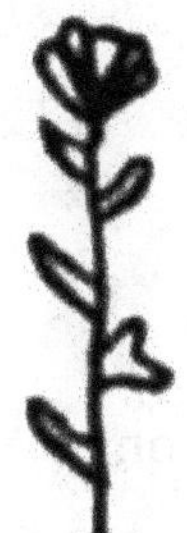

Lemon

You're sour,
You're bitter,
You're an off-brand lime.
You're a lemon.
The plain, The sour,
Bitter taste.
We spit you out
because of your lies
and the dirt you threw on us.
You're a lemon
That nobody wants.
something bitter,
sour,
Meaningless.
To me your just a lemon.
A lemon,
A lemon that is thrown out when we please,
Squeezed when we please,
Cut up when we please...
You're just a lemon to me,
To me...
You are a lemon in pain.

Washed Off On Me

I saw you just earlier.
When you walked through the door
I was hit by a spell;
I almost fell to the floor.
When I see you I get nauseous,
When I think of you I almost faint
'Cause I think you washed off on me.

Meat

I was used to the cuts.
it's pathetic I know,
it hurts in my gut.
You only fall for the next man who breathes.
I don't take things I don't own;
You borrow and steal.
The first kiss is a seal.
I’m not just a piece of meat.
I have feelings too.
I have a touch too.
I never gave too much.
You used me as an object,
Played me like a violin.
I hope you find a piece of meat,
Just one that isn't me.

Glass Half Full

I filled my cup,
To the top,
so no one could reach me.
I learned a lot from spending time away,
I felt happy knowing I was safe.
I found the key to my own heart,
I found the treasure inside.
I fill my glass half full,
so I can breathe a little easier today,
I used to fill it to the top.
Now I fill it half full,
To let others in.
If I can love myself,
I can love others too.
I want to give,
I want to love.
So I fill my cup,
Half full.

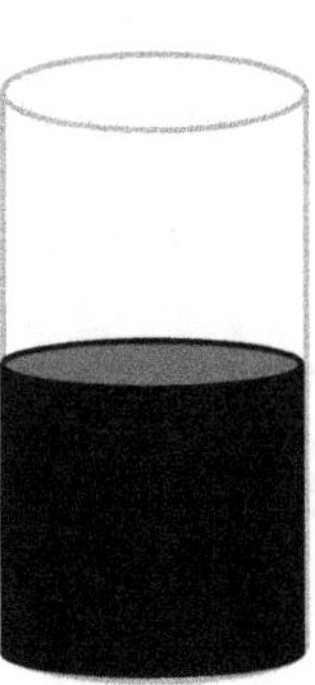

Can't Eat

I starve most days,
I can't live most days.
Most days,
I live in a place
... it doesn't feel like home.
I'm not happy here.
It is very clear.
I can't eat.
it's not a choice I make,
I just can't.
it's not a choice,
I just can't eat.
Even if I wanted to,
I can't.
I won't.
it hurts,
but I can't just give up.
I just can't eat.
I can't eat.
I really wish I could.
I can't.
Even when it hurts,
I can't eat.
it hurts too much.
To give in hurts even worse.
I won't.
I can't.

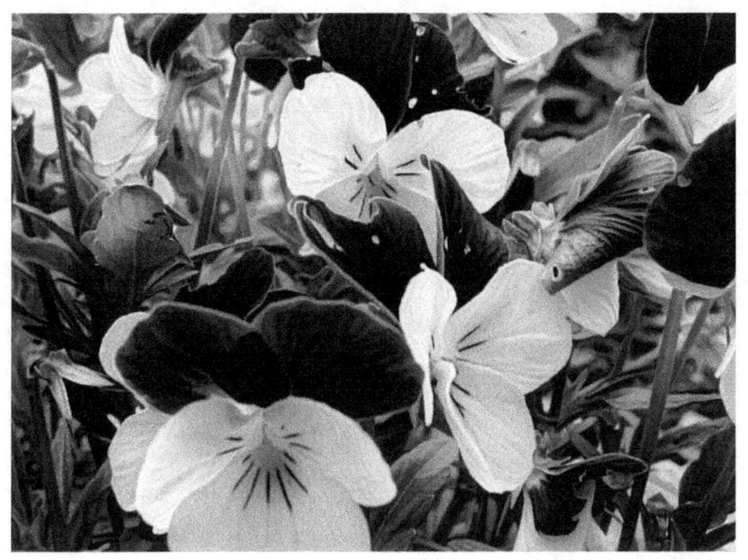

Chapter Seven
Mess

Tongue Tied
7
Tulips
Letters
Ainmosni
I

This is my problem.
This is my mess.

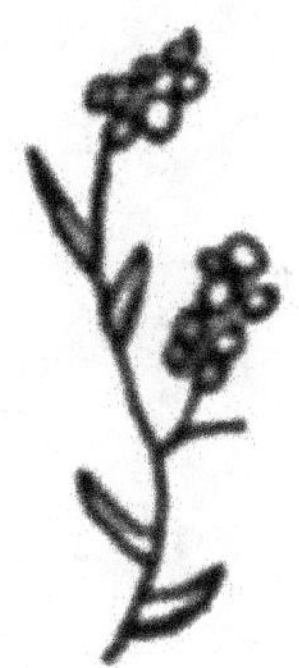

Tongue Tied

Can't spell,
Can't tell,
Can't yell,
This isn't going well.
I got tongue-tied.
Can't get out of this mess,
This happens often.
I guess I have no luck.
I’m tongue-tied with you,
and I can't fix it.
Yes, I’m tongue-tied.
I hope it wears off,
Like a fever.
I’m tongue-tied and I can't wait to speak,
because I’m in love with you.

7

I am a little disoriented,
I am gonna get help,
Don't worry.
I am a bit worn out,
but so is everyone else.
I am a little distracted,
Don't worry.
I am just tired,
Like everyone else.
I am sick of the reliability on someone else,
Just let me do me without consequences.
You love me,
You hurt me,
You touch me.
I am a little under pressure,
Don't worry.
I am a bit worn down,
so is everyone else.
I am a little hurt,
Don't worry.
I am gonna find my way out.

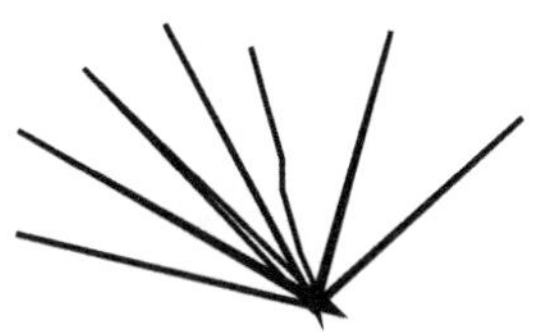

Tulips

Gardens of sorrow,
Tell me is it tomorrow.
How can we move on so fast?
How did the tulips grow without you?
I don't think you meant to leave,
but this is a part of the seasons.

Letters

I could have sent at least one,
but I just read them all and sent you none.
You tried to send me letters
I wish I did not receive.
I cry whenever I open them,
I'm happy when they're gone.
I could have sent you a letter,
but I just didn't.
I didn't have the power
To even send you one.
So now I'm sorry,
because you're gone.
I wish to know you
I wish to love you
I send my love.
I can't send a letter.
I wish I would have,
but I just didn't.

You sent me all those letters
I wish I did not receive.
It's not that I'm ungrateful;
I just can't open them.
I can't send one back
because I have no words to say.
All I know is that
if you were here today
I would hold you tight
and never let you go.
I cannot resist
Another letter you sent.
I can't send one.
You sent me all those letters
and I wish I did not receive
but I will open all of them
With hope for you and me.
I Love The Way You Lived
How you treated me
I love the way you try
to hold me together.

Ainmosni

I fear loss,
I fear love.
I hold it all in,
and shake it off.
I cry at night
when no ones
watching me,
I have problems sleeping...
I can't sleep at night.
I fear the moon above,
I'm scared of the dark
and all of the thoughts.
I know I am safe,
but darkness hurts.
Can you help me up or not?

I

In my beginning,
I have had many problems.
Many. . .
I have had White lies drown me,
I have had lovers fool me.
I had tried to escape this darkness
but it still continues...

Chapter Eight
Unloved & Undesired

Words
she says
Colors
Lost
Paralyzed
Honest

Lost, honest, no words, she says your hands paralyzed me, her walls cover her wounds, I see colors through those mirrors.

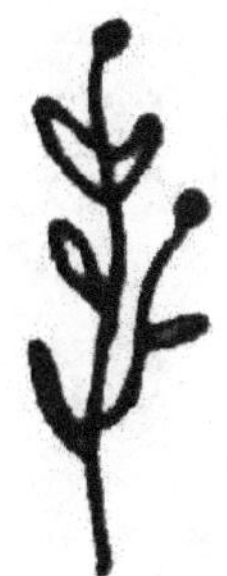

Words

These words hurt,
These words give.
Words are a weapon,
used in love and anger.
These words are a penalty.
They bring sadness.
They are just words,
but they give and hurt.

They can't kill us,
but they can damage us.
These words,
Our words,
Affect all the people around us.

The words,
They hurt,
They love,
They bring you up and down.
My words give and love,
Your words kill and hate.
Our words destroy each other.

Why are words hazardous?
Why are words glorious?
My words will give and love.
Our words will love
and change the people around us.
Words love, Words hate, Words give.

she says...

she says I love her
she says I care
she says I want her
she says, She says...
she says *I love you too*
she says *I want you*
she says *give me your all*
she says, She says...
she says *I need you*
she says *you're all I have*
she says *give me more*
she says, She says...
she says *I cry for you*
she says *I call you*
she says *I would run to you*
she says, She says...
she says *I have to leave*
she says *I never wanted love*
she says *I used you*
Now he says, he says...
He says he loved her
He says he cared
He says he wanted her
He says, He says...
she says "*I never stopped loving you*
but I just don't love you anymore"

Colors

Colors show beauty.
They show you.
They show me.
Red for a rose I gave to you,
Yellow for the sun on my face,
Green as the grass I lay upon,
Blue as the sky above,
Orange as the fruit I eat,
Purple like the starfish in the sea...
but these colors brought me to
beautiful you.

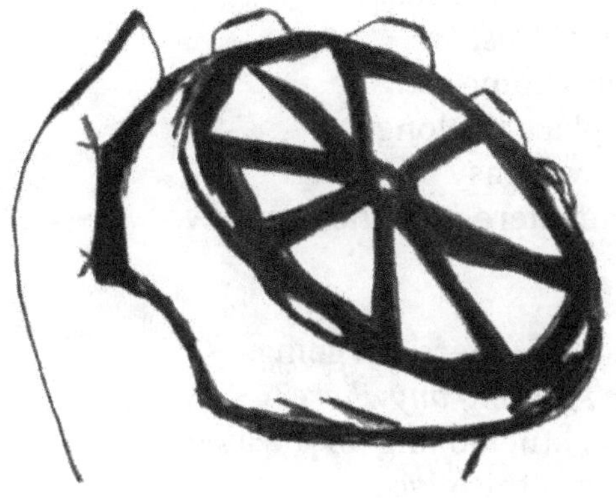

Lost

Am I lost?
Am I lost?
Am I lost?
I run through forests,
I climb up mountains,
but I am still lost?
I can't find home
or someplace I belong.
I wish it was easy
like somewhere over the rainbow...
but no,
I am lost?
I don't know where I'm going.
How am I getting anywhere?
How am I still looking for a way
to get out of this place?
Maybe somewhere in outer space...
but I'm lost?
I'm lost?
I'm losing my mind?
I'm not always okay,
but I am lost?
I don't have a place,
but I am lost?
so lost.

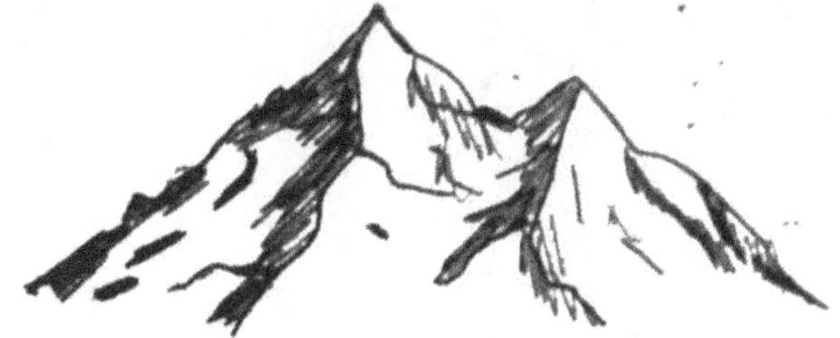

Paralyzed

Loving you changed me.
Loving me gave you a reason to stay.
Loving you gives me chills
but you paralyzed me.
You put me out like a flame,
You changed who I am.
Loving you is hard.
Loving you challenges me and my heart.
Loving you made me better
but you paralyzed me.
Now I am held captive in your love.

Honest

If we had just been honest,
We wouldn't be fighting right now.
I know it isn't all your fault,
but it isn't all mine either.
If we had been honest from the start,
We wouldn't be wasting our time.
I don't want you to leave.
Love, just be honest,
Do you really love me?
Do you desire me?
Just be honest with me.
I call you up because I want to,
I want to care for you.
I won't if you're not honest with me.
If you don't love me,
Leave.
If you don't desire me,
Leave.
Love, believe me,
I want this.
I don't want to be unhappy though.
Can you just be honest?
It's all I ask of you,
Besides you loving me.
Just be honest.

Chapter Nine
Paper People

Believe what you can until you crumble

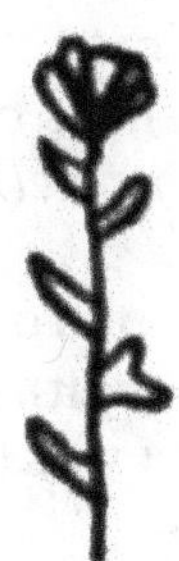

Stupid Angel

Stupid angel still crying,
It wasn't easy lying.
I know you're sad but I'm pretty glad.
I know I'm not in your shoes but damn,
why do you have to be so cruel?

I left before it got to the pits of her flames,
I didn't want to go down with you and your shame.
You seem to forget that I was the only one who was there.
You also know I was pretty scared,
So why do you have to be stupid, you angel?
Why do you have to be such a mess?
Why do you have to break my heart over and over again?
You were good, now you're bad,
Why did you hurt me like that?

I gave you a hand up before
and now I needed your help.
You couldn't help me because you still hurt.
Why do you have to be.....
Such a stupid angel with me.
I don't know how I can reverse time
but I hope you find what you're looking for.
I just know...I know...that it wasn't easy lying to you,
I knew you would cry....so I said goodbye....without a word.....I am not sorry for you.
I know you still hurt.

Moments I Live

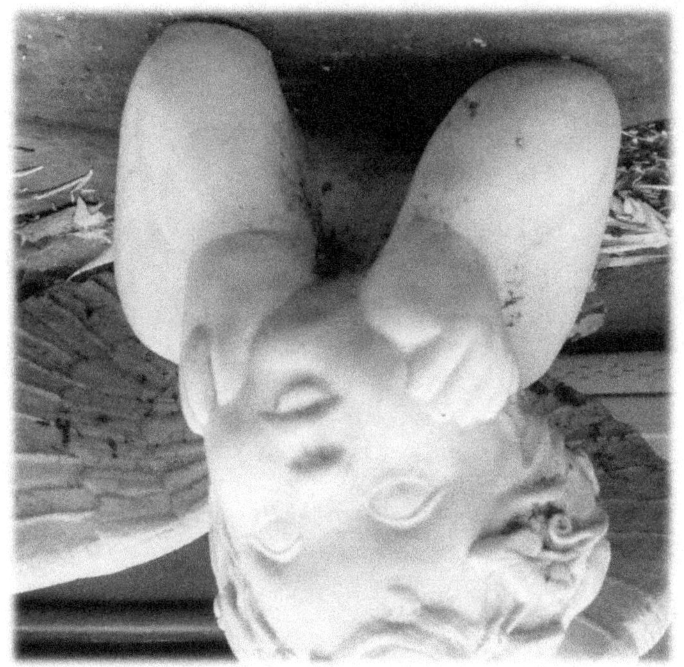

if

if they could have seen how high we were.
They wouldn't question why we broke apart.

Darndest Things

Now that I am older I hear the strangest things.
I hear that I am smart like it's a bad thing,
I don't want to be the bad guy.
You don't know what I feel like.
You say the darndest things to me behind my back,
yet I'm listening.
I hear your toxic hurtful words,
yet I still forgive the one.
I don't want to feel connected to your energy, you say the cruelest things behind my back with a knife in your hand.

I can't stand the constant hurtful painful words you spill on my food.
I can't hold onto the little unspoken cruel things you hide in your head.
I don't want to hear the words you speak while I'm listening.
I know you don't care about my feelings but if you're happy then be happy.
I can't hear your voice in the wind now that I silenced the one.
You can say the darndest things to me behind my back, yet
I'm no longer listening.

Paper People

Torn,
Crumpled,
Ripped apart,
Cut in pieces
... Those Paper People did this.

How will my friends understand?
Those Paper People tore me,
Threw me away,
and got away with it.
I hide those Paper People in my closet,
Those ones who hide in the dark.
Paper People can't-fool me now.
How is this my fault?
I can't stand their hopes and dreams,
Their little problems with me.
Those Paper People are hurting.

One of them took my heart to play,
The others just watched in awe.
They don't understand my pain and sorrow.
They cut me open with their scissors.
Tore my heart in half.
My friends try to glue it back together
but it can't be repaired.
Those Paper People
won't leave me alone.

They watch my every move.
They don't understand.
They are everywhere.
They can't help me.
They are not my friends.
Those Paper People...

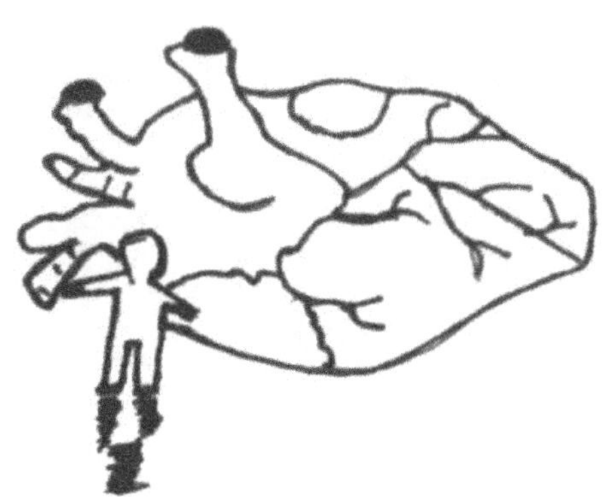

I'm done.

Insensitive I know.
Save your advice for someone who is willing to care.
I know what I want....
I want to heal.
Can't you just let me sleep in my cocoon...no you must barge in when I make a small amount of noise.
I know that I want to walk but I can't with you dragging me down.
I want to heal but you won't let me.

tell Me so

Tell me so I can give you my heart further,
Tell me so I know how to show you love,
Tell me so I can love the magic within you,
Tell me so I do the right thing,
Tell me so I spend my time on you,
Tell me so I care about small things you say,
Tell me so I cry when you're gone,
Tell me so I love the earth of us,
Tell me so I give you all the edges of me,
Tell me so I can live on after you're gone,
Tell me so, one more time.

Paper Airplanes

The bell rang and released us to recess...
I saw them playing cops and robbers.
I walked up to them then asked if I could play.
Elijah said to me "walk away you FREAK"
So I walked away for more than a week and
They would have let me play if I had a cool T-shirt
but I just sat alone
in the same blue sweater with nothing better to think about.

They watched Ben grab a piece of paper and as he folded it up to take his fire at the only kid who had nothing but a lighter to protect him from the airplanes he glared and yelled a cruel word.
I guess they don't know any better.

but my mama said...
They don't know you and
Kids can be mean and you'll make it through because you are clean.
I know you'll do the right thing and keep flying.....

Red paint on my hand and everyone thought I had hit Ben
but what they didn't know was that they all hit me first like missiles.
They aimed their airplanes right at me and they let go on the count of 3.
Their airplanes hurt me.
They had cut me down from my landing.
They made me fall from the big blue sky,
Never knowing why I deserved it.

but my mama said...
They don't know you and
Kids can be mean and you'll make it through because you are clean.
I know you'll do the right thing and keep flying.....

but those words didn't help me because the kids made me want to sleep...
So I gave up on my dreams,
because they weren't "manly" enough for them.
They threw their paper airplanes at me,
They flew Through me,
and cut me down.
They never knew what it did to me.
but I should have known better
Then to ask those kids to play.

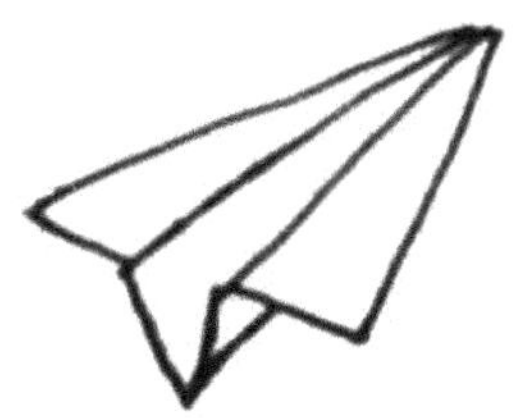

4

Days pass with no act of violence.
Anyone can be the victim.
You said yourself that I played the part;
Venom is your drink of choice.
Individually we walk with the tag on our backs.
Dare to pay the price of your sins.
I can't pay the price for all your sad goodbyes.
Very little shame in what you call friendship.
Anyone can see that you haven't heard from me.
None of you will find me, I'm tucked away hiding.
All of your lies only hurt you.
Now You say it's my fault.
Getting further away from the truth is never easy.
Everyone knew your secrets.
Leaving me in your closet was always the plan.
Joke about who I really am.
Own your actions, You will go farther.
Everybody knew that it wasn't your fault.
You ended up holding it in and telling nobody.

II

I am afraid of what is next;
these years don't go away. . .
I am melting from inside.
They can't help me!
Nobody can. . .
I must struggle alone and...

Chapter Ten
Nightmare of Myself

Circus Show
Reputation
Doctor Heart
King of Lonely
Moonlight
Nightmare
Stranger
Tear Bear
Me, Myself, and the Moon
Colorless Eyes
K
Tear Bear PT.2
Nightmare of Myself

BELIEVE IN YOURSELF OR DARK DAYS WILL FALL.

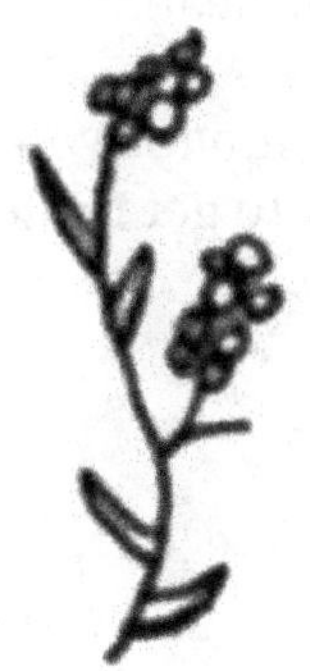

Circus Show

Clowns dancing around your house,
Fake crown upon your head.
Hold on for your life,
Tonight is going to be fun for you and me.
There is no other way to get to sleep,
Enjoy the circus show.

Reputation

No promises but I will be here,
for you.
Don't look at the little things like you do,
My love, this has been fun but you could do better than me.
I know that our love has been burnt and your heart is softly falling apart.
The hearts in here pull all your strings up and down.
I like you when you're broken too;
I can't make any promises but I will be here.
My reputation has never been this tarnished in the eyes of the man.
It's so cool that you still love me and I love you too.

Doctor Heart

Doctor heart
Answer me this:
Why do I feel this?
Why do I care?
Why do I need it?
Doctor heart!!!!
Why is it torture to me?
Why can't I love another?
Even though I know that she can't love.
Why? Answer me.
Doctor heart,
Doctor heart,
Tell me she is hurt.
Tell me she can't stand me.
Tell me she wants me.
Tell me she cares.
Tell me she loves.
Doctor heart,
Can you answer me?
It's not hard to answer.
Doctor heart!!!!!
Just answer me this!!!!!
Why does it hurt?
Tell me,
Doctor heart.

King of Lonely

I stand up,
and then get pushed down.
They add pressure to the pot,
I always stand upon the heat.
I am the king of lonely.
I stand alone,
I fight all alone.
I am alone,
and nobody is home.
I am poor me,
and cold in the heat of day.
The pressure holds me,
Holds me to be lonely.
I am the king of lonely.

Moonlight

I'm standing in the dark,
Right next to you.
I feel like holding your hand
right now.
You feel that moonlight.
That's the light of our skin,
The touch of love, You see.
The moonlight is in our hands.
We're just standing in the dark.
Together the moon shines,
Alone the stars fall.
The moonlight has me.
Sleeping forever...
This moonlight is broken.
Can you feel it?

Nightmare

Can't wake up because I am lost
in a terrible dream.
I want to see the new day, please.
They look for your deepest fear,
The one they call a nightmare.
The creepy-crawlers of the night,
The hidden faces you see without the light
... This wouldn't be a nightmare without you.
It will make you never want to sleep,
... That's the nightmare that gets you.
Only you can scare you,
This is your nightmare.
This fear of sleep keeps you up at night,
and that's alright.
Don't think of it anymore,
This nightmare is only temporary.
The haunt of a scarecrow,
The scare of a sad clown,
An old cry of a night mime
... This nightmare
in the night still haunts me.
A Nightmare is you.
A Nightmare is......is us.
A Nightmare is what I created.

Stranger

Heartless souls over the bend.
Don't bury the hatchet.
I can't give her up,
I fell in love with a stranger.
I am underneath a trance.
I am falling under the pressure.
She has me playing all her games.
I told you I was hurting,
and I can't give you up.
I know it won't be good.
I fell in love with a stranger.
Her anger hurts me.
someone send me away from this hell.
She haunts my dreams still.
Take me to the good place instead.
I fell in love with a stranger.
I am underneath the ground.
someone send me a God.
It can't get me out of this hell now!
it's killing all that I know!
it's killing what I am!
I cry and scream because I fell deeply in love with a stranger from hell.

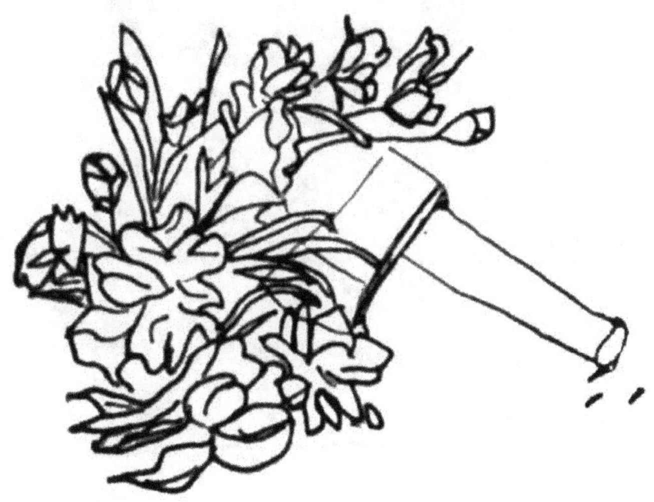

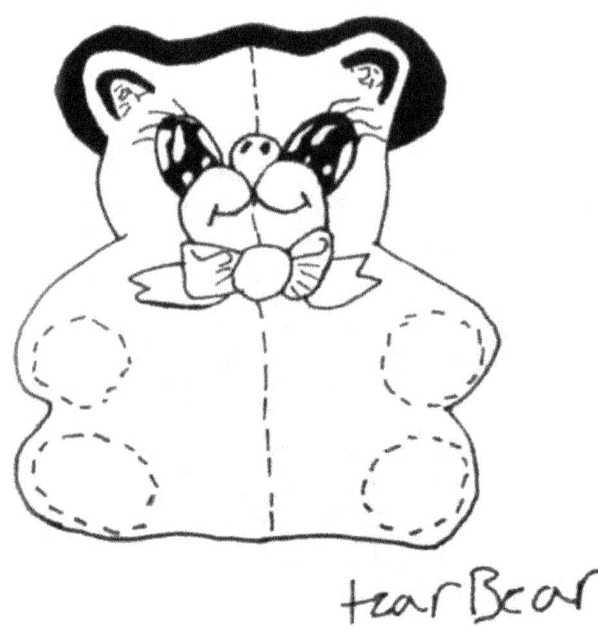
tearBear

Tear Bear

I carry their tears,
I hold them close,
Until they need them. . .
They called me their tear bear.
I just hold their tears in bottles.
Never are they wasted,
Therefore, I am here.
Tear bear is the name I was called.
I carry tears to cry,
I carry cries from long ago,
I carry sadness in the back of my mind...
I have never lost a tear,
Not even one.
They called me tear bear.
The one in your saddest moments,
The one who cares but can't speak to you.
I'm just a lonely tear bear.

Me, Myself, and the Moon

ME.
Me not always happy,
Me Never saw the light.
Me can't live without love.
Got no point in living anymore.
Me can't keep giving my soul away.
Me can't seem to open my eyes.
Do you know how Me feel?
Have you ever lost your mind?
You never get the right one back.

MYSELF.
Myself is trapped,
Is lost,
Can't even breathe.
Never am I true to myself.
Myself can't hide the truth.
I have never once given up on myself.

THE MOON.
One side in the dark,
Another never sees the light.
Pulled around,
and has a few craters in its heart...
it shines in the darkness.

ME, MYSELF, THE MOON.
Me is here,
Myself is there,
The Moon is above.
This is Me, Myself, and the Moon.

Colorless Eyes

You see the world black and white.
You hold onto the little things
that don’t matter and that's alright.
It's okay to be upset,
but when you can't see the color
the color I made with lilac soul
you turn your back to me with your colorless eyes.

With you it always blame me,
Always put down with your gravity.
Spilled graffiti on my broken heart,
yet you still can't see the marks you left.
Oh, your colorless eyes they leave you alone in the
dark.

K

I don't know how to feel now
I don't know what you're doing here
I don't like that at all
I don't want that from you
and I don't see anything with you and me.
Why does love ruin me?
Why does it deceive and defeat me?
Why does it hurt me?

Break me,
Break my pencil,
Break my heart.
You don't know what you hurt,
I know where it began to scar.
I just hope you know,
I don't like your love,
I don't want your hands,
I don't want any of this,
so leave me alone!
I don't want to be lost,
I don't want to feel confused,
I don't want you!

You play with my emotions,
You walk away without a scar.
It's for you,
It's all for you.
Why can't you see that?
I don't like that,
I don't want that,
and I don't see anything with you and me.
Why does love ruin me?
Why does it deceive and defeat me?
Why does it hurt me?
Why does it hurt like this to me and you can walk
away with everything you started with.
I don't understand, why do I feel like this?

Tear Bear PT.2

I moved from box to box,
and shelf to shelf. . .
Nobody knows what I have held.
I had to carry their tears until the end,
Nobody knows what I have done for them.
for sitting on a shelf,
I sure did a lot.
I was the one you held close,
Now you throw me away,
What the hell did I do to you anyway?
I have sat in your house since you were born,
Now I am nothing more than a stuffed bear. . .
I held you when you cried for me,
Call me tear bear. . .
That's what I'll be.
I will move from box to box. . .
To shelf to shelf. . .
Just so I can see where life takes you.

Nightmare of myself

My nightmare ended in blood,
I was the one who had done
the unthinkable.
I had killed the nightmare of myself,
I was forever scarred by the face I made back to me
after dark.
I couldn't breathe after that party was over,
I in pain for seeing my own death and witnessing the
sorrow of losing me.

I couldn't help but scream
in the streets of New York
for help when I was in my own dream,
Nobody could hear me like reality.
I still ended the nightmare of myself,
I was no longer breathing.
I awoke in sweat and tears of witnessing that
nightmare of myself.
I went to wake my face with water,
I fell through the bathroom tiles.
as I knew this was still a dream for I was lost in a
maze of darkness and blue leaves on the ground as
the fog was above and as I crawled so I was not seen.

I must wake up from the nightmare of myself,
I just want to go home.
There's no place like home.
I want to go home.
There's no place like home.
I wish for home.
There's no place like home.
There's no place like this nightmare.

Chapter Eleven
Life of Doubt

To face death without fear is to live without hesitation.

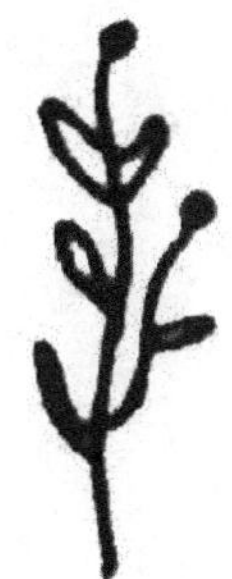

Live Tonight, Die Tomorrow

Why live,
Why die?
Just because I cry
Doesn't mean I want to die.
Just because I say love
Doesn't mean I mean it.
but I'm living tonight,
Then I might die.
I need a new lover,
I will find you.
I'm living tonight,
Then I might die.
I need love
in this little town.
I need you,
and I need you a lot,
but I'm living tonight.
Then might die.
So love me for 24 hours,
Then forever give me flowers,
but I'm going to be living tonight,
and dying tomorrow.
I'm gonna live tonight,
Then I might,
I just might...
... but I'm living tonight.
Then I will
Die tomorrow.

One Lie

Can you tell me how?
Can you let go?
Can this be true
or is this unreal?
but the sky is crying.
They see what I have done,
They see what I do,
They know who I have hurt.
The sky is crying out.
The sky sees us lie.
but why does the sky cry?

L E S S

C o u l d   c a r e   l e s s
a b o u t   y o u r   l o v e .
C o u l d   c a r e   l e s s
i f   y o u   l i k e   m e .
C o u l d   c a r e   l e s s
i f   y o u   s e e   m e .
C o u l d   c a r e   l e s s
i f   y o u   h a t e   m e .

Paint Me a Picture

Paint me a picture
Of your mistake.
Paint me a picture
Of our lives.
Paint me a picture
Of us.
When I see us sometimes,
I get emotional inside.
so Paint me a picture
Of love.
Paint me a picture
Of hope.
Paint me a picture
Of you and I finally happy.

Key to My Heart

"You have the key to my heart."

but how did I do that?

"You just did."

She unlocks who I am.
I turn the key
To make our love smile.
She is the key to my heart,
The one who loves me for me.
The only key to my love lock.

??

Are you gonna be here in the morning?
Will you stay the night one more time?

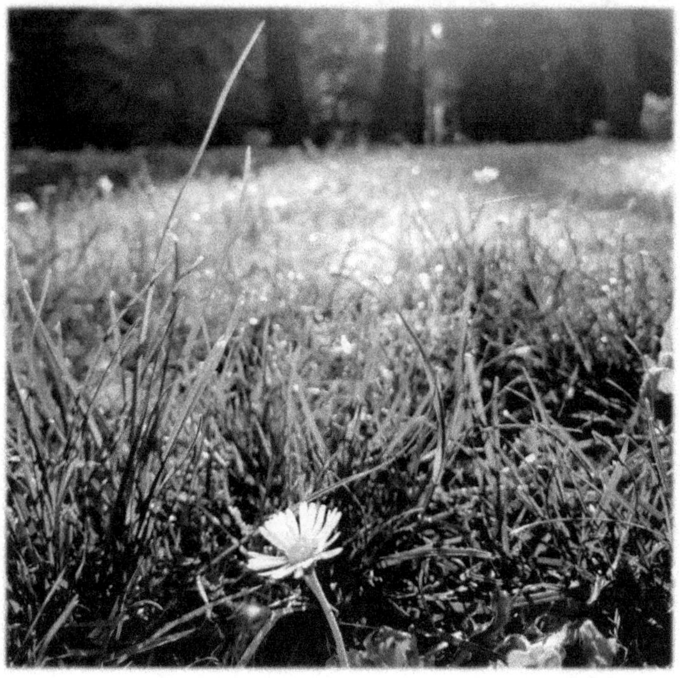

Doubt

I doubt you love me.
I doubt you care.
I doubt you are honest.
I doubt you tell the truth.
I doubt you ever loved me.
I doubt you are living,
I doubt you have a soul.
I doubt your eyes have color.
I doubt you see me.
I doubt you,
I doubt us,
I doubt everything about this.
I doubt we will end up happy.

N e v e r

I always thought about me.
I never had trust in us.
I always thought it could maybe work.
I never knew I could love someone like you.
I always thought I was broken.
I never knew.

Runaway

Racing for your freedom.
Unity is all you have with yourself.
No one can know where you are.
Accidents happen on this journey.
Waiting is scary in the dark.
All you need is love but you have nothing.
You will keep running away.

Moments I Live

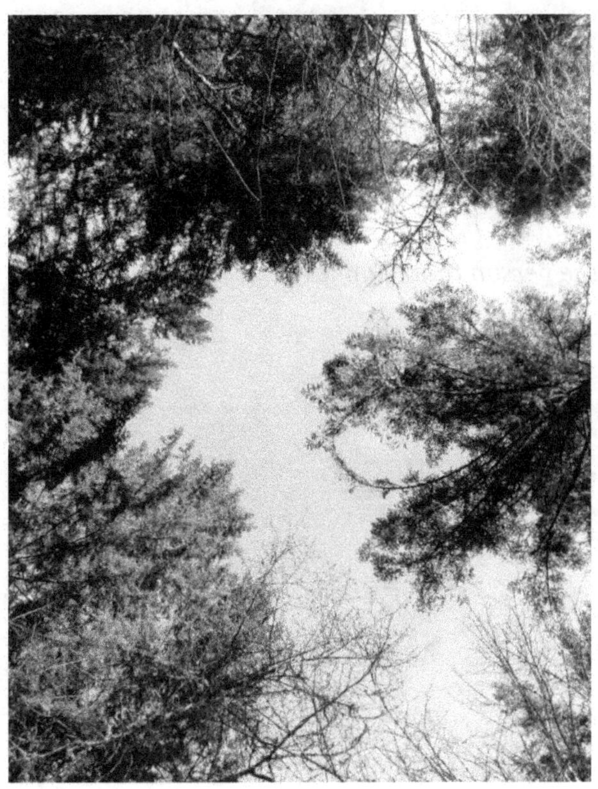

Chapter Twelve
Changing for You

I See
Tell Me How
Dressed Up

Be the person that changes someone for good.

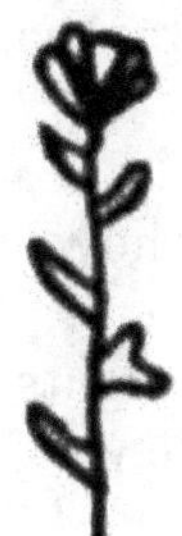

I See

on that day I wish,
I wish I could be there.
because now I see what is really there.
am I blaming you?
am I blaming me?
the world never knows how I see.
I see the things in color,
I see the things in dark nights,
I see what my mind believes.

is it what I remember?
is it what I imagine?
is it what I need?
no, but it's what I see.
I see myself happier,
I see myself better,
I see myself as one with me,
but is it what I saw before?
is it what I wanted to know?
is it what I really want to see?
is this me?

because I seem happier,
I seem better,
I seem to care more than my usual self.
so if I ask myself today
to see the best of me...
to see what I see,
is to be very careful with reality.
but I once was very sad.
now I am filled with all new things.
this is what I see.
that is all I see.
but *what do you see in me?*

Tell Me How

(Instructions: please handle her with care)

Tell me how to understand you,
When you don't act like yourself,
Tell me how to know when I'm wrong,
When you know that you're right,
or when I get mad in the night,
Tell me how to take care of you,
When you're injured or hurt inside,
Let me be the one to say it first,
When you can speak no words,
When you lose yourself,
Tell me how to handle it,
but before that,
Tell me how to love you right.

Dressed Up

I get anxious around you,
I get butterflies in my room.
I don't know what to do,
You just seem to know.
So I am gonna dress up for you,
I am gonna show up for you.
I am gonna be here for you,
Let me love you too.

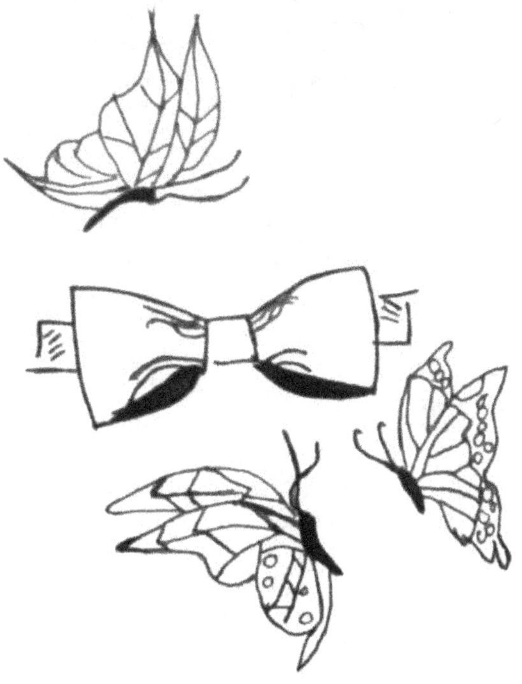

Chapter Thirteen
The Flame of She

Everything is Okay
Gentle
No mercy
Flame

Be who you are.
Be your best self.

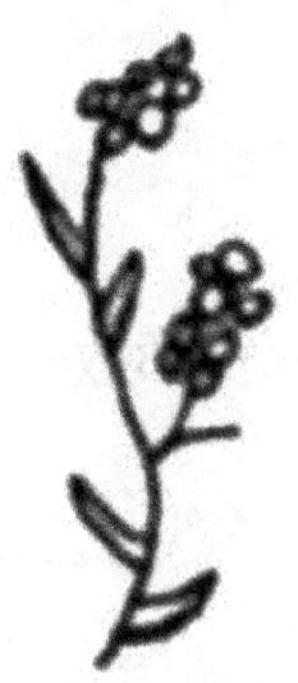

Everything is Okay

I’m scared,
Not prepared.
You're here,
Next to me.
I see that
You understand,
but you say everything is okay.
When it's not.
but it will be.
Not all is perfect,
but you’re by my side.
You just say everything is okay.
You’re not always okay,
but you make it out alive.
but you say everything is okay.
but is it?
So think everything is okay.

Gentle

Leave my reputation, in the dirt.
I keep you in my thoughts some nights.
It's better than living in lies.
You wanted better, so I apologize.
Love always has a big surprise.
Our love has some dirt upon the surface.
The dirt covers me because I have been the bad guy.
I want you to love me so gently
so That it won't hurt you or me.
I want it so delicate,
so I don't bleed.
I won't be a careless love you admire.
I want our love so gentle,
so that it won't hurt if I left you.
You want love so soft,
so I don't cut your heart open.
All I really need is for you to trust me,
and love me so gently.

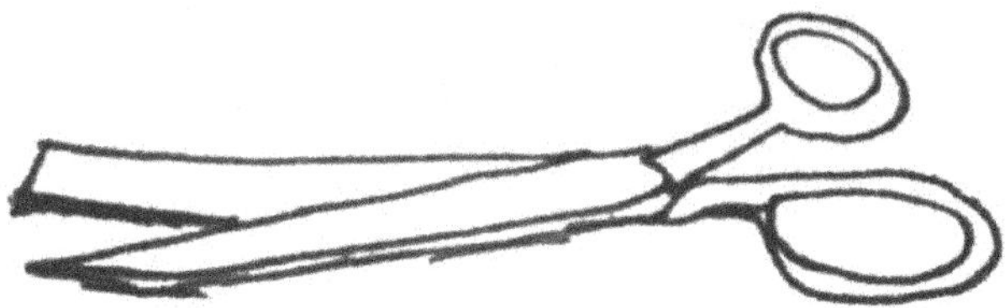

dear unknown,

i dont want to live like this,
i dont want to feel this way.
you can break me down,
to the lowest point.
i know life has no mercy,
i need somebody.
somebody to tell me,
life doesn t care.

sincerely,
sunflower

Flame

Candle wax upon my fingers,
Little do I know it's yours.
I don't know how to take it,
How do I take it?
Can I put out your everlasting flame,
It shines too bright next to my face.
I wanna touch the light,
but yours burns me.
Shines like the sun,
Dies Like the wind.
Hold me tight,
Don't let me go when I fly.
See you again soon,
I want you to know I wish the best for you.
I will be happy too,
but my flame is gone.
You blew out my candle.
I left the lid on too long.
Your candles are gone,
and I am moving on.

Chapter Fourteen
To: self

Top of the World
Cough Syrup
Best Part of Love
Love is What it is
I Am To Be What You Want
FAKE
Masking Tape
Bad Guy
Life, Light, Me
Dear Body

"Nice Advice Lives inside"

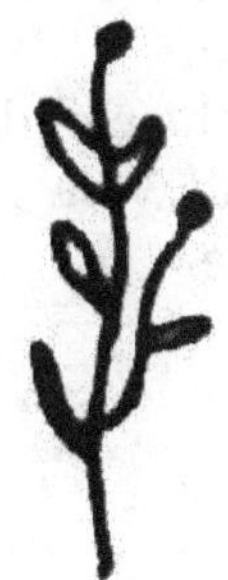

Top of the World

I just wanna feel on top of the world.
Climb the stars to get out of this world.
Just need me and my soul
to jump hoops through the clouds.
We need to travel far and wide
but I want to be up there.

Cough Syrup

Your heart hurts and you take it out on me.
It's so easy for me to leave,
Now that I know.
Who could ever know your soul like I do?

I bring my mind to those thoughts,
Again and again due to you.
I have been the cough syrup,
Curing your sickness.....
and *this is how you treat me?*
Who will be there now?

Now that you burned your ways into my life,
You want to predict my future but you'll never know...
You'll never know how much I use to love you.

Best Part of Love

The best part of Love is getting to know somebody...
To know that someone will love you.
To know that they care.
To know that they will be there.
To just see them act on what they say they're going to do.
To just hear them say that they truly need you in life.
I am not saying that love defines what a person does as being real love,
I am saying that if somebody puts your best forward for you, they truly love you.
The best part of love is understanding that people care.

Love is What it is

Love has failed me more than twice,
I don't know if I can sacrifice anymore.
I had to give up so much already.
Freedom.
Voice.
Myself.
How can one say they found true love again?
Why do we act surprised when it ends?
WE HAVE ALL SEEN IT BEFORE.
Love is what it is and that's it.
There is no end.
No beginning.
Only you and a form of magic with another.
Love isn't what you may think.
Trust in yourself that you can define real love.

I Am To Be What You Want

How can we help one another?
When we are all so broken.
You look to me, I look to you. . .
but no one knows.
It's not that I hate everything and everyone,
but I can't stand the people that hold me back and take any chance they have to get what they really desire.
I am to be what you want.
I am to see what you need.
I am to be a part of your life.
I am to be nothing more than a friend.
I say this now,
I am to be what you want but I am not going to be something I am not.

FAKE

How can I be something I am not?
If I can change to be what I want to be like,
Then why do I get called fake,
When I become something, I am not to please you. . .
Why am I ashamed?
When I become fake to be
better than who I was born to be.
I admit that I can be a bit much for you...
I know that I still seem fake to you.

Masking Tape

Little problems always grow.
Seeing me above afloat,
Was so traumatizing.
I guess I want to see the ending,
but I know a person that was here.
He was kind and gentle.
He saw things clear,
I haven't been myself lately.
Tried to hide it from the public.
Tried to get over it,
but maybe it's time I just end me.
My fake personality can take over.
So nobody will bother me.
I can't hold myself up anymore.
I have drowned from all of my past,
I guess I lived through it all,
I fell asleep and never woke up.

I ended my life at least a few times,
Since then I was never the same.
I saw friends as achievements,
I saw the people that hold all my differences.
I can't hold the mask on anymore.
I can't wait to see again.
They won't like what they see,
They found my secrets beneath me.
I have problems,
I'm aware.
Thanks for nothing but hurt.
Thanks for nothing but hell.
I needed more from me but what the hell.
I couldn't live in a place I wanted to.
I couldn't hurt like I needed to.
I couldn't be me if I wanted to.

Bad Guy

All happiness has ended,
It all faded to blue in the sky. . .
Tell me was it ever really real?
Tell me did it mean anything to you?
Tell me was I a waste of life for you?
Tell me was I ever really good for you?
I know I must seem like the bad guy.

Life, Light, Me

Holding onto life,
Staring at the light,
Looking back at me.
Knowing life goes on,
Sitting in the light,
Hopefully, you know me.
Hoping life is light for me.

dear body.
you may have cracked interior.
but you re not broken completely.
you are beautiful
and made neatly.
love is hard to find within.
is that why you share your skin?

you cant change your structure.
you cant bend the bones.
you can inject yourself with poison.
but that cant change how you feel.

someone must have decided you were
perfect.
because you seem to smile when they re
around.
you may have lost touch with me.
but i am still around.

love you is all you need to do.
care for the skin upon your bones.
life is short. live long.

just when things get bad.
think about how much you did before that.
you carried all that weight on your back;
growing up isn t that bad
nothing should stay sad forever.
past can hold you down.
let the ones you love protect you now.

love your skin and your mind.
love yourself. dont be blind.
carry on with your doubts.
all of this will clear out somehow.

sincerely.
mind

Chapter Fifteen
Bumpy Ride

Introduction . 51
All the Way
Bicycle
Take it From Me
Shatter

It will always be a bumpy ride with you.

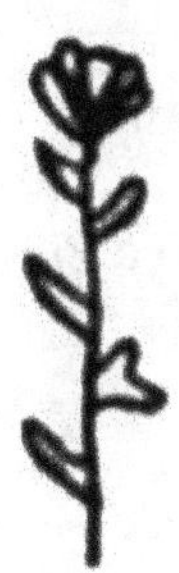

Introduction . 51

One, Two,
I'm Still Thinking Of you.
Three, Four,
you Walked Out My Door.
Five, Six,
you Crushed My Heart To Bits.

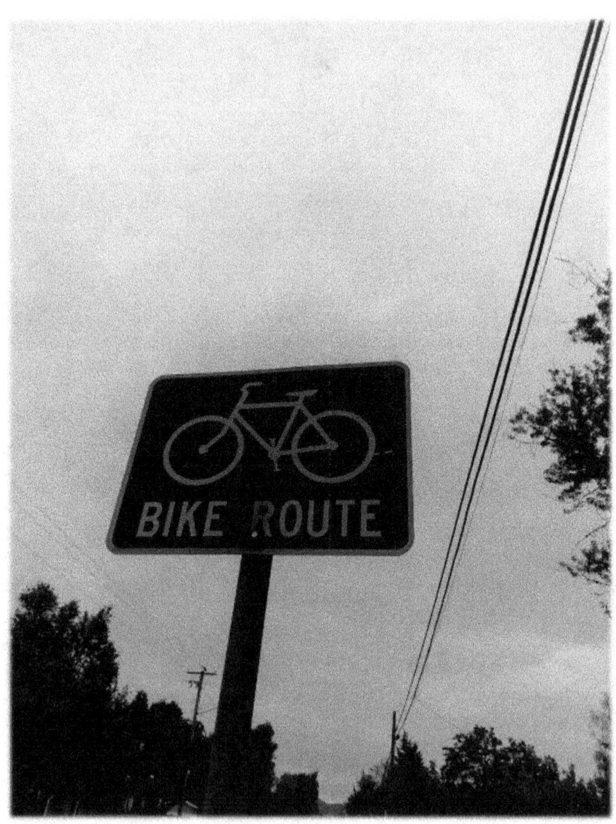

All the Way

We may cross a certain path.
This isn't close enough.
I push you away,
and you come back,
and you always want more.
You wanna go all the way.
You can't quit this love,
This mistake on your heart.
You call me yours,
but I don't feel different.
but still wanna go all the way.
I say what you want to hear.
You wanna go all the way,
but I don't want to.
I don't feel close enough.
You're like a stranger.
You can't be hooked on me;
I am not in love with you.
So don't make me go all the way.
but you just want me.
All the way.

Bicycle

Take the next exit if you're scared.
I ride on two wheels.
I care about who you are
and where you wanna go.
It's important that you know me.
Let's just ride,
Ride this love to the end,
Only on this bicycle.
Do you love me,
When I'm here and when I'm not?
Do you wanna go like I do?
We can ride this bike to a new place.
Scream if you wanna let go.

Enjoy the ride till the end.
I wanna do this right;
No problems or mistakes.
This is special.
Let's ride the bike on some training wheels.
We can ride until we are gray and old.
We can ride our bikes in heaven,
as long as I'm riding next to you.
We only know where we start,
Never where it will end.
It's just you and me on this bicycle.

Shatter

Don't push me to the edge of life.
Shatter me if you want.
I'm standing right in front of you,
so do it now.
You say I hate you
but that's just not true.
Now you've broken my glass
and I'm heartless on this cloud.
You broke my heart
to those shattered pieces.

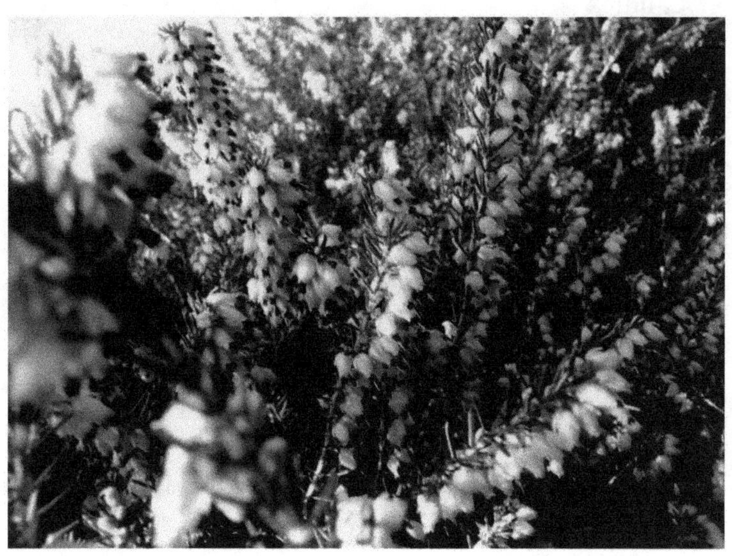

Chapter Sixteen
Alphabet City

Masks
Sunflower
Ink
Hostage
Patterns
Civil War
10
The forgotten
Prince of the Owls
Candles
Strikes
Red
Alcohol
Frighten
BYE
SNAKE
Pages to Fill
I was you once
Tears in Hell
Carousel
Blossom Lips
Alphabet City

Welcome to Alphabet City, where dreams come true...

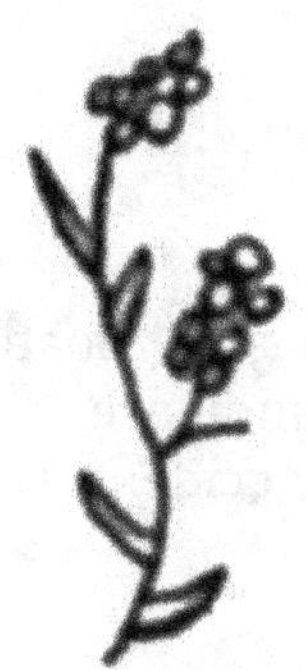

Masks

Wear them,
Keep them until death...
These masks hide self.
They never show the interior.
Hush. Don't speak.
Don't even blink.
The masks are always sugar-coated but never are they honest with the audience.
I play the part of The Accident, The Victim, and The Hanged Man.

Sunflower

My heart's petals have fallen.
I can't be sorry for this,
It just means I have to go.
I have to end it.
I have to go,
I can't be here.

Ink

Permanent.
Bleeds through the skin.
Ink is tattooed on my heart.
Every time I blink,
You get closer.
Just one drink
Before we go...
This ink in my heart is poisonous,
but I guess I like it.
This ink just bleeds through my skin
like love for you takes to give.
This ink sinks to my heart
With every little thing.
The ink on my body is why you can sink into my soul.

Hostage

Say what you need to
just don't say you're leaving.
Make a life with me in paradise.
Can I keep you as my hostage?
Can I hold you, when I am alone?
I taste salt in the air,
The point of no return to rise soon.
Keeping you with me
is the reason I reach for heights.
Can I keep you as a hostage?
Let me keep you here.
Let me hold you in the dark
in the light of day.
Can I meet you here?
We could keep each other hostage,
Only if you want to.

Patterns

Follow your rules and
Control yourself.
You keep lying to yourself like it's easy.
You always lie,
You never lie,
Your pattern never changes.
You have your same tricks,
You always go back to them
when you're done.
You never look before you leap,
You follow your patterns of lies.
Can you see how this makes me feel?
Can you be honest like you promised?
Look what you did.
You went right back to where you started.
That's where we parted forever.

Civil War

Divided,
Destroy and conquer,
Torn apart...
Pieces of a civil war.
Civil war breaks you,
Civil war tears you up.
It changes a person.
I see it in your eyes.
The civil war started here.
It will end soon,
but only time will tell.
It can only bring hell.
but when one man falls,
It is a new game.
It is a new world now.
The civil war changes how I feel,
It changes how I live,
How I love, Who I love...
... it tears you apart
but no one cares.
Only the kings dreaded its end.
Only the queens decide who dies.
but this is a civil war.
This is the fight I have within every night.

10

One girl,
Lives in a small town.
Isolated from the hurting people.
Very shy in the outback,
If she falls to the dark side. . .
Anyone could get hurt.
Held against her own actions,
as a warning to be silent.
SILENT
as she drinks the cold glass of pain,
She holds the fear in her eyes.
To break loose of any pattern,
Only she can disguise herself in white.
Read the title of her name.
You will feel too.

The forgotten

Thrown out of society,
Different types of anxiety,
The world doesn’t accept me.
We are different because we are beautiful.
We are children of a God
but *why must we be forgotten?*
Why can't the world be shaped for us?
I don't want to be the joke anymore but
we are pretty in ways most aren't.
We care when others don't,
We are there when others aren't,
We try when others don't
but *why must we be forgotten?*
Why do we not achieve warmth?
Why, God, did you make us this way?
Why be beautiful
If I feel ugly?
Why be here
If I’m forgotten?
Why live when I’m not needed?
Why is the world against change
and why are we forgotten?
Why am I alone?
Am I the only one of the forgotten?

Prince of The Owls

Carry us,
We follow,
Guide to the sky,
Never leave a person behind.
but *do you love us,*
Prince of the owls?
Lead us to the sky,
Lead to the heavens…

Prince of the owls,
Do you care?
Lead us to be free,
Lead us to be us,
Never give in to hate.

Prince of the owls,
Do you see?

Lead to true sight,
Lead to better light,
Never hate one another.

Prince of the owls,
Do you cry?
Lead to the mountains,
Lead to the river,
Never burn the Earth.

Prince of the owls,
Do you believe?
Lead us to a God,
Lead us to good,
Never leave a person behind.

Candles

I'm just waiting
but you never call.
So I light these candles.
I lit them up to get warm
because you're not home to cure my cold.
These candles go out 1 by 1.
I don't know how long you have been gone.
Still, I'm waiting
but no call,
so I light these candles to mourn your cold.
I just think I might fall into sleep alone.
I'm growing tired of waiting.
Never thought I would want you
but I want you home.
I watch these
Candles go out 1 by 1...
You're still not home.
No call.
so I light these candles.
These candles burn my skin.
When I'm without you,
I'm lonely and so cold,
A brokenhearted fool
but I still light these candles,
Still just waiting for
you.

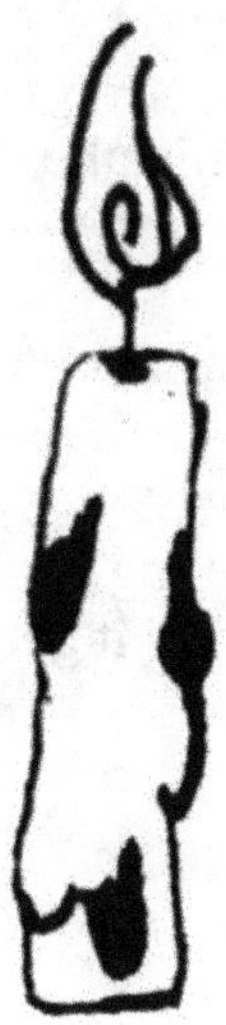

Strikes

1
I forgave you for your mistake,
Then gave you love you don't deserve.
I gave you my all,
I showed you new things about me...
Nevertheless,
I can't be without you.
Don't blame me for striking you out.
Five strikes are as good as it gets.
2
I kicked you out.
Now I hate you,
Can't stand you,
but I still love you...
I don't want to,
but I do.
Five strikes are as good as it gets.
This is how you want me,
Then love me for real.
3
I can't believe you.
You're at it again,
but this time it's my best friend.
I see you, but never again...
I think you are stupid.
Five strikes are as good as it gets.

4
This is on my nerves,
This is only on my terms now,
This is personal to me.
How did you get my weakness?
When did you love me like this?
but five strikes are as good as it gets.
5
Last chance to love me right,
but you still won't do it right,
Not even for one night,
Not when I want to...
This has gone on long enough.
You know my rules.
Five strikes are as good as it gets.

Red

I hate you so much.
I dislike you to a point like no other.
Your fire roars from within your heart.
Your own life was at risk.
You still can't resist that color of red.
The one that I hate so much.
You wear it as a scar of our relationship.
I hate you so much for hating me for leaving.
Wasted my time, you did.
Your hate for me is strong
but my hate for you is stronger.
I hate the color of our love.
I hate that shade of her,
but I hate myself for ever loving her.

Alcohol

Open up a bottle,
Cry a little,
Say a little,
Drink some alcohol.

Alcohol.
Yes,
I remember you coming home late,
but I didn't mind.
I treasured you
but I didn't think I wanted you.
I wanted this though, I can't lie about that.
Alcohol solved my problems at the time.
Alcohol loved me when you didn't.
It was there
When I was home alone.

Frighten

Her eyes are no different,
Closed or open they are the devil's.
I hear you talk about me,
I hear her voice that poisons the room.
I don't like her,
nor do I like you for talking with her.
I want her to drown in the blood of my wounds,
I want you to move on.
Why can't I leave the past behind me?
Why can't you get over being anything with her?
I need you to know,
From now on I will hate you.

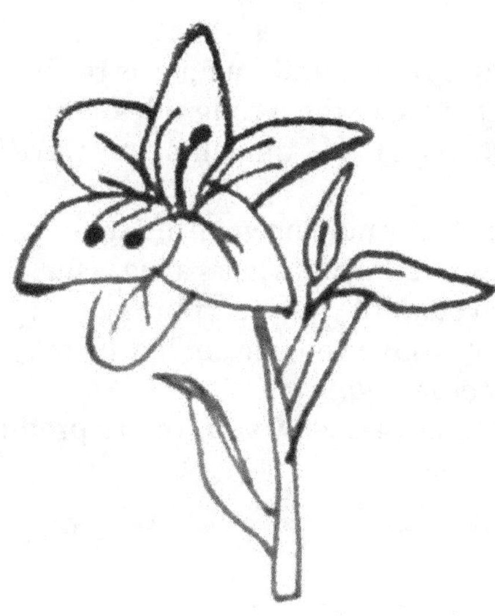

BYE

Breaking out of your domain was the hardest part.
You pulled me to the wrong side of the street.
Even when I had my thoughts they were always wrong.
Forgive me for making your life so much harder.
Evil lives within you, That's a big issue.
Life thrived until your heart broke.
I'll never forgive you, for not letting me go.
Can you ever change?
I'm never surprised by you, You're predictable.
Again I say bye.

SNAKE

Cheater.
Liar.
Theft is a crime.
Stop selling her secrets for love,
Stop telling her shame for something new,
Stop being such a snake.
You think she doesn't see you,
but she does.
It hurts me more than anyone,
Shedding your skin doesn't change you.
Can you please let her go?
Take your poison out of her heart,
So she can feel again.

Pages to Fill

I have pages
and pages
To fill.
They all have memories;
I hold them close.
They are the ones I love the most.
but I have pages to fill,
Memory slots to fill,
Snapshots and baby pictures,
Pages and pages...
someone told me,
To live is to never give in to hate.
That page is still unfilled.
I can't fill pages with hate.
I can fill them with tears and letters each day that I
wait for the truth.
some days are forever,
and some you wish to be forever
but these pages I fill will all end.
I still have pages and pages,
and still, pages to fill
Until the day I smile and die.

I was you once

I was a timeless heart waiting to be discovered.
I was the one you thought you wanted to be.
I was the man of their dreams.
I was in love as sad as that seems.
I was in the same seat.

I once had the energy for negativity
but now I don't see the reason for denying their poisonous opinions.
I once had time for toxic love but now I have had enough.
I once wanted more than this but now I see what life had to give.
I was you once before all this.

Tears in Hell

Devil or not,
Demon or god,
I cry in this hell.
My tears burn on my cheeks.
I don't see pain,
I see anger.
I feel rage,
Feel it course through my veins.
I cry in hell.
My cry for help.
I can't even yell,
The silence is so loud.
The quiet hurts,
The flames burn,
The people run and I stand and cry.
These are my tears in hell.

Carousel

Our love is strong,
I feel it.
but *how do I know you won't let go?*
We go round and round...
... This love is like a carousel.
The love we hold is like sweet cotton candy
but we don't know where it begins or ends.
We go round and round.
We are never close enough to say love.
We never get our thoughts out to each other.
Our love is like a carousel.
We never know when to stop.
This love,
Our love is like a carousel.

Blossom Lips

... Nice evening in our hands...
We see the stars above.
We want to get close,
but we don't want to fall.
Do we want this,
or *will you leave?*
... Got to be home before 2 A.M....
but all you want to do is watch the sunset.
Why can't we get close?
When will I see if our love is true
or *just pretend?*
These stars are lining up the chances.
I wish I could be brave,
So I hold your hand tight.
Then I press my lips on your blossom lips,
I opened my eyes and you were gone.

Alphabet City

Alphabet City is a lost cause.
Lost people walk the Halls of death.
Trapped souls, Oh, poor souls are here in Alphabet City.
It's so close to being gone...
I don't remember the last time I sang the song.

How it happened was so magical,
I do remember how this town came together,
Where it began in the center.
It started with a voice.
A sweet and sad boy he was,
Who lived alone
in this worn down city.
He wanted to change the days of pain,
He needed help to carry this city up.

This city is glamorous,
Now he that he runs the show.
He is in control of the magic beyond.
That sweet and sad man
is the life in Alphabet City and will live on forever.
His heart so pure that it plays in Alphabet City.
He is the man who made Alphabet City.

Chapter Seventeen
Imagine Me

Introduction . Took it To Far
Painted Glass
Follow
Close Your Eyes
Imagine You Out Loud
I Can Be
forget Me, forget You
Buried Town
Shameful
Bury the Truth
Played
Interlude . What Am I, a Fool?
Lonely forever
Let Me Know To Leave
88 Keys
Lay me Down
Beautiful Lies
Happy
After That
Outroduction . What is me?

Imagine me just floating away happily for once.

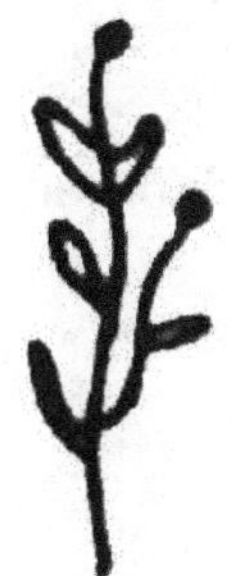

Introduction .
Took it To Far

I am the one who said it.
You blame me.
Why am I here?
How about we leave each other.
forget about me
and I will do the same.
Is it too late?
To say we took it far?

Painted Glass

The light from your window seeps through onto your skin.
The glow of the red and yellow make me want to believe in happiness
but I know it is not possible for me.
I hurt most days
but your color always seeps into my dark days to make them better.
I just wish you liked me enough,
so we could be together.
So I can be the one to tell you,
You are a masterpiece.
You have the color I have been looking for
but in the end, I know,
I will still end up alone.

Follow

I hear your voice.
In my head is where you are.
I feel nothing anymore
but *are you near?*
Are you close?
Can you hear me?
I want you to follow.
I want you to go with me.
I want it to be perfect.
but with you, **nothing is**.

Moments I Live

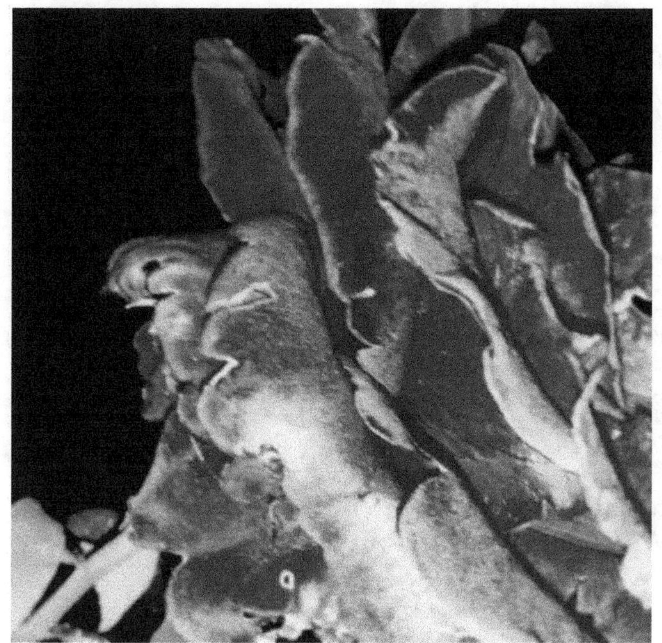

Close Your Eyes

I have a wonderful idea.
Take your time.
Walk with me.
I wanna see all that we can do.
I wanna imagine that you're still with me
and I just wanna close your eyes.
So I can imagine you here with me.
Close your eyes and think of what we had.
Close your eyes and dream of me.
When do you think of me?
I have been wondering,
Do you think of me?
Have you thought of how I feel now?
I want you to close your eyes and imagine us together.
We walk this road before the end of time.
I want you to know
that I will always be here for you.
I want you to let me be free
because when I close my eyes and sleep,
I can't help but want you next to me
So I can breathe a little easier.
I want to be better
but *who am I kidding?*
I can only hurt myself
because when I close my eyes,
I think of you.

When I need time,
Just know it's only for you.
I want you to know that I loved every second that we had
and I want you to know that this isn't over yet
but we can make it go faster
because I need to let you go,
so I can finally move on.
It's been a while
and I know we haven't got long.
We only have this life together;
Let's make it the best.
Close your eyes and think of me
and I will walk away from you.
You will not follow,
because you are stuck.
I am not real,
So how can I be there for you?
I wanna be there
but I know now that it's ending
and I know that my world is spinning.
When you close your eyes and dream of me,
I want you to know that I can't wait to see you once again
but you know that when you close your eyes and think of me,
I will be there for you.

Imagine You Out Loud

I think about you
more than I should.
You're like clouds forming before the rain.
You create a storm in my brain.
I only ever say your name out loud.
You seem to forget what we were.
Now I don't regret seeing the end.
I can't compare you to them.
You're broken inside
and burned outside of your frozen skin.
I imagine you out loud.
How do you appear in this world?
I imagine you above.
How are you here?
Why are you here?
I seem to imagine what you used to be.
Now you're like a beast within me.
I let you out when you haunt me.
I can't control the things you do,
So I imagine you out loud.

I Can Be

I can be selfish,
I can be needy,
I can be your love
or the concept of it.
I can be darkness
or the good parts of it.
I can be worthless
or worthy of all the colors.
I can be me.

forget Me, forget You

I wish you would come and save me.
I wish that you would want to imagine me.
I don't know how you really feel but please forget me.
I will do the same.
You can get rid of the pain in my heart
but I can't find you, so forget about me.

Buried Town

It's much too late for me.
I am stuck outside reality.
I daydream, and I never know what to do with my life
at this moment I have.
I seem to remember a place below,
A place once above that had a glow...
It was the main attraction.
It was what held up our town.
It is now a buried town.
Nobody really cares
about what happened there
but I know that's where the trouble began.

Shameful

I guess you didn't know;
You didn't get my phone call, I guess.
I have no words;
They're stuck somewhere.
It's been a while since I've been lonely;
I guess I haven't heard from you either.
I need to know if I am to blame.
I need to hear your heart beating.
I didn't know how much I imagined us.
I didn't know that this was so shameful.

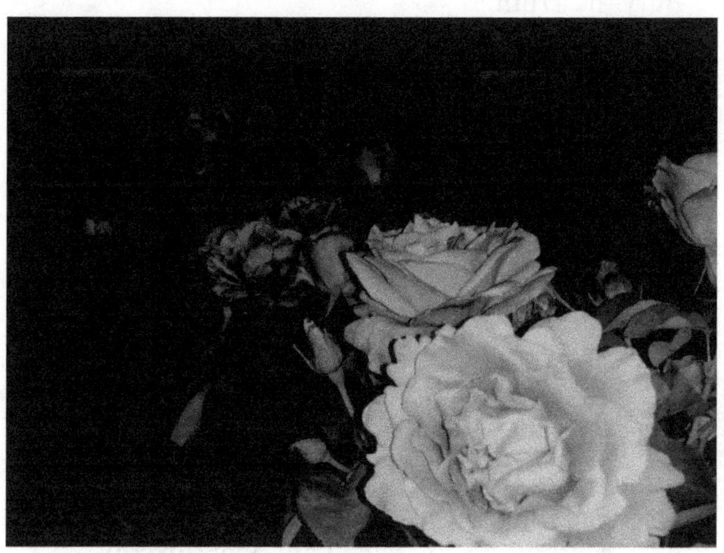

Bury the Truth

The fire was lit outside by the baseball field.
On that Saturday morning, I knew that everything
could alter in my **universe**.
and I finally knew what I wanted.
I wanted nothing to do with what I wanted.
I had no reason for living a **lie**,
No reason to love or cry...
I had only reason to lie like a child,
hurt like a crying wolf,
and bury the truth in my **own** backyard.

From that moment I knew that I
could not escape my life of **misery**,
My life of sorrow
or to continue life knowing **I am heartbroken**.
It's not something I am proud of being.
I do not have the cause that makes me this way
but the **truth** hurts, so bad nowadays.

One by one my friends and I march out to the field,
The field like the fire within me.
I had no idea that they really **imagined me.**
They saw me as content and cold
Like a cloud that covers the sun.
The one that could believe in hope.
Was I that hope?
but as I thought this out loud,
They kept digging away,
as if the truth had been corrupted,
as if they saw what I finally saw:
That you have to **bury the truth** to move on.
I can't imagine a life without any lies,
Any *poor you* or *you're a bad guy.*
I can't imagine a world without conflict,
A world in which we are the same.
So as I watch my friends march with their shovels,
I march away into the forest to become known
as truth.
I could be their truth and their **false words**.
I could show them the lies that protect all of
humanity.
I was **the messenger bird.**

Played

I feel like asking for too much
but when I do,
I know it may seem excessive.
I know I may act out a lot
but I know that it's always my fault.
So sorry if I fall.
I don't wonder this at all,
but *have I been played by you?*
I know it seems crazy, but have I?
or have you ever lied to me?
I know I have just asked for free.
If that's our problem, then I guess you can leave
because I only want what I can afford.
So if you let me in,
I guess I am sold.
You were never good at poker
but *have I been played by you?*

Interlude . What Am I, a fool?

Why did I go with you?
How could I remember this?
I am nothing right now.
I got an idea:
Can you just let me free?
Am I just a fool?

Lonely forever

I can't deny any tension between us
but I know when we got close,
I was the only one who ever got hurt.
You never took me seriously
and after that, I think you're dead to me.
I am left to the side a lot
and I expected more from you.
You don't like what I wanna do.
You expect me to be a part of all of the things you do.
I don't think I will go out tonight.
I think I am too hurt by you.
I don't want to pressure you, or anyone
but I think you need to push me over.
I think it's time that I get over you.
I know it's hard,
so I will make it easier for you.
I think we should part ways.
I think that you need to move on,
Like I need too
and I know from now on,
I will be scared of love.
I know I will be lonely forever,
Only forever.
I wanna be alone like a single coin,
The ones that rust after rain.

You know when we get close, I get comfortable
and that leads to me fading.
but I know now,
I am better off lonely forever.
It's only forever.
What if I choose to stay?
What if I choose to be with you?
but I know I am better
If I am lonely forever.
It's only forever.
I know me better than before.

Let Me Know To Leave

The candles I light are for her.
I know you don't like it.
I know we have made it before.
Why now, when she is gone?
She is gone, and I know I am a little obsessed
but I miss the sight of her.
I miss her voice in my head.
Can't you forgive me?
I know you hate the speech I gave at her passing.
Nobody makes you stay
but *would you let me know to leave?*
I know, I put you through hell.
It's a lot for me.
I admit that it is my fault.
I know that it hurts when I don't forget her.
I am a guy with lots of problems.
You are so understanding.
It's so nice to know you're here.
You have been there for me
and I have been hurting myself
because I know it hurts you.
Admit it this time.
Just know I only do it for attention.
but I want to tell you this...
Let me know when to leave.

88 Keys

How can you say that we were wrong?
You never said you couldn't play.
There isn't one key that I won't play.
You played lower than I thought.
I played with every key I could.
You told me that I was so wrong.
How can I be wrong when I played all eighty-eight keys
and you never played three?
How can you say that you love me?
When you never even stayed?
How is this supposed to play when I am sitting here
alone?
Why do I play every key on my own?
You can pretend you don't care,
You can say you missed a note
but you really only missed me.
How can I be sure if you won't go running?
because *when you close your eyes, Do you think of me?*
When you say my name, Am I all you see?
I know that you never played me,
as I played you with everything.
I played every key from one to eighty-eight and I
never once stopped to breathe.
Was I what you hoped?
or am I missing a key?
I may not be beautiful all the time
but I play just fine.
I wish you knew how much I cared about you, as I sit
and play eighty-eight keys for you.

Lay Me Down

I crossed my arms for the last time.
I know it has been a long time
but I just wanna live,
I wanna feel,
I wanna be better for you.
For you, I was waiting,
For us, I was fixing.
We can't fix each other
If we don't want help.
I am alone now,
Buried six feet too far.
You can't save me,
so save yourself.
Lay me down somewhere safe.
Lay me down where you know I can't escape.
I want you, but I can't have you.
I know you live outside of the city,
Near the Old Creek.
I want to flow through that stream,
but first, lay me down.
I don't want to lay just anywhere;
I want to be close to you.
Lay me down where I can feel,
Where I can live,
Where I am safe,
but close to you.

Beautiful Lies

Can you hear me now?
I want you to know that I miss you.
I don't know what I want anymore
but I know one thing
is for sure:
I loved your beautiful lies.
They sounded so sweet,
Like lullabies.
Can you tell me what I did wrong?
Was I wrong to hurt you?
Was it all my fault?
I don't know what I want anymore,
but this is for sure:
I miss your beautiful lies.

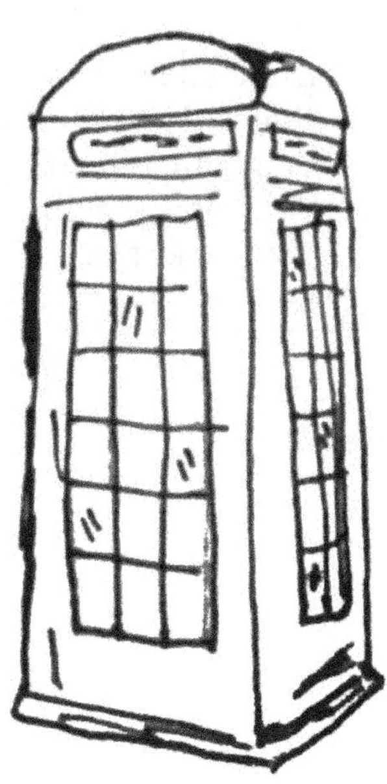

Happy

I can only fix myself.
It's not hard to say that now.
I guess I never knew
How I could imagine you there.
How is it so fake for me to say?
They see hell,
I see heaven.
Why did I not see it coming?
You knew you would leave.
I had no clue that I could fall so far.
I just imagined you so well.
I was up in the stars,
While you were creating a new hell.
I felt my room crashing down on me.
It was all like, *I know you are not happy.*
It was all up in my imagination land.
How can I not see that you could hurt me?
How did you know how to get me?
You pulled the trigger at a point.
You know you did it.
You never returned to stop my bleeding.
I know happy is not you.

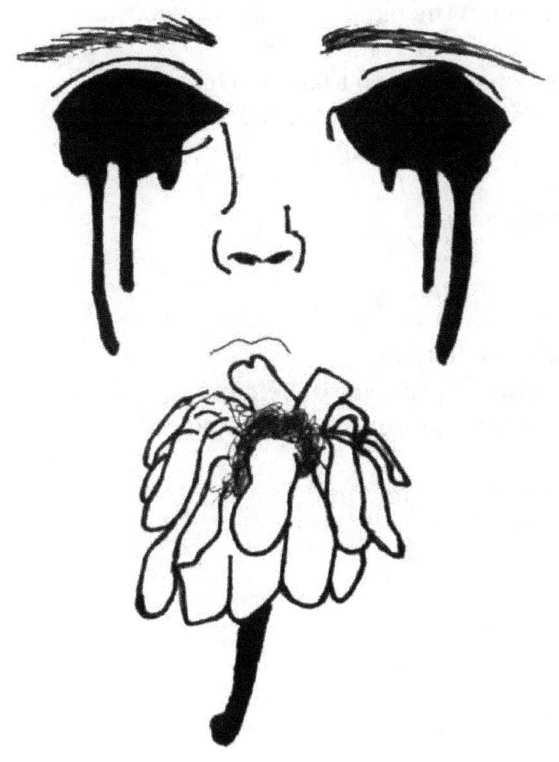

After That

Tell me all of the bad things about you.
The one before left me in pieces.
Please leave, so I don't fall in love.
After that, I am lost in your love.
Just imagine me trying to escape.
I can't.
Can you imagine?
I can't.
Can you help me?
Can you?
Nobody can help me.
Nobody has the power to help me.
No medicine is strong enough, and nobody can solve this.
but after that, I am done.
End of story.

Outroduction .
What is Me?

Had to take some time away,
Forget about us.
It's over, and you knew it.
I knew that I was sorry
but I am now gonna leap into darkness
and hope I come out alive.

Chapter Eighteen
His Playground

Under the Bed
Killing Yourself
Whisper
Hide and Seek
Death Wish

Join the shattering silence on his terms.

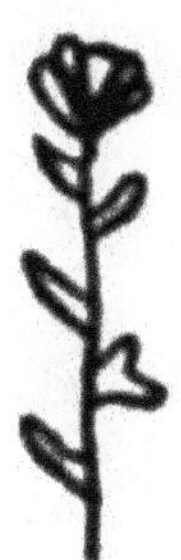

Under the bed

Don't look under the bed
There are some secrets to find down there
I hope you're ready for it now

Killing Yourself

Cold in your bedroom;
Did you think your mind couldn't find you?
Tossing in your sheets,
Trying to get some sleep.
You still manage to kill yourself.
Blood flooding your mind again,
Still changing throughout time.
You can make it,
You are strong,
You know you can't fall and give up this time.
You need to just breathe,
Walk with me in your mind,
Hold my hand,
I have survived.
You can walk the road too,
I have hope for you,
I have light for you,
and you have everything to survive the night.

Whisper

I
hear you cry for the ghost,
I
know you want to love me.
My heart beating so fast I can't hear,
The *whisper*
that is haunting me.
Can anyone help me?
Maybe my friends
will understand...
Can you hear me calling your name?
I hear you in the dark of the room.
I'm near you.
I feel it.
I whisper for you...
I laugh in **sanity.**
This is my reality.
The whIsper haunts me.
The ghosts all fall silent.
It kills me
that no one *understands.*
It's my whisper.

They hear it
too,
it haunts them
too.
The ghosts **scream** in panic.
Maybe now they understand.
The *whIsper,*
how it calls me...
Will someone help me?
You hear it call you
every time you move.
The whisper haunts
you.
The whisper ***sees***
you,
it calls your
name.
The whisper of the night
Never shines bright,
But it calls my name.

Hide & Seek

It's hard to breathe with all the dust.
Why do I seek while you hide?
This isn't fun for me.
Why can't I have it all?
The only time I see your face is in the pictures.
I always seek while you hide,
So come out,
Come out, wherever you are...
Let's play hide and seek in the dark.

Death Wish

You wish,
You wish,
You push,
You push;
You want it all.
I can't give it all.
'Cause girl you have a
Death Wish.
This is me,
Giving you mine.
Now you lose
The Death Wish.

I try to give more,
You cry and take more.
I don't get it.
Lose the Death Wish.

Chapter Nineteen
Real Friends

Real Friends
Cries and Lullabies
Boys in the Trees
Painted Heart
Preschool
Real Friend

Unconditional love is what I expected

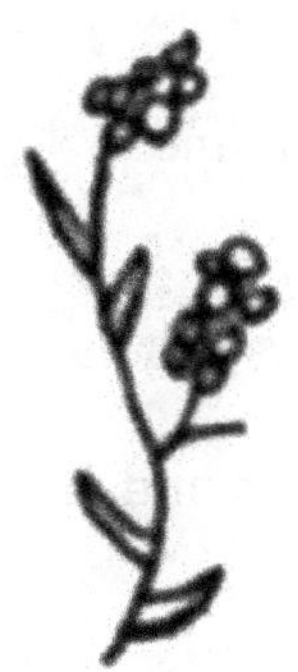

Real Friends

I don't know
who my real friends are.
I can't see
what lies beneath the name.
They can't say
I didn't try
to be honest.
I don't want to be
the one who trusts them and falls.

Cries and Lullabies

I save my goodbyes,
I don't want to cry,
but I just might,
I sing this song for you.
Before you go,
I've been thinking about you...
I sing my lullabies,
and hold my cries,
I'm gonna miss you
like I already do.
I hope you're happy,
Even if I feel nothing now.
This is so sad to me that you're going.

Boys in the Trees

You see me
but let me be.
This is easy,
I know how you are.
I understand how much you care
but you hide with the boys in the trees.
You understand what I do,
You get how I am in brutally honest with you,
You are my support too,
and I care about you.
So go hide with the boys in the trees.
You don't need to help me get on my feet,
Even if I just take defeat,
but I understand if you want to be with the boys in the trees.

Painted Heart

Colors fly...
They fade too.
They cover up the dark
but it's more than that with you.
More than colors and shapes,
Swing sets and friendships,
but *what is it?*

What are they?
The ones who stand out,
The ones who give in,
but never run away.

It's us,
It's me.
The ones who care,
The kindness in the heart,
Those beautifully painted hearts,
On the wall.
Will they ever fall,
in deep love?

Preschool

Playgrounds fading into the sunset,
Paint still drying on my fingers.
Waiting for Mom or Dad to pick me up,
The other kids are already gone...
Tomorrow I will be locked up again,
In this jungle with savages.
I have no freedom,
Inside these walls.
When I leave,
I think I am free of fists in my face.
At least I know now,
The bullies on the sidewalk are gonna follow me
home.
They're going to shoot their BB guns,
as I walk in shame for being to young.
If I was older maybe they would like me.
I am a kid, I fall and have to get back up.
I know I can't change me and
no band-aid can fix the past,
I learned that back in preschool.

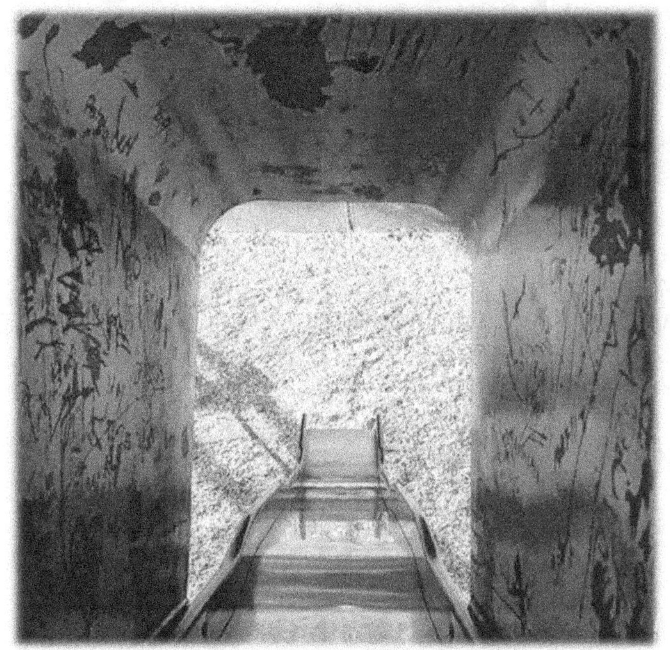

Real Friend

My heart was a frost,
Just like my eyes.
You seem to have grown up,
I loved you before that.
I know you're happy,
I know you hoped that I would be free.
I don't know why
but you're always here for me.
When I am all alone,
I call you on the phone.
When I need you the most
and you need someone close.
Even when I run,
You follow me.
So why do I hurt myself?
Why do I hurt inside?
I have you
but I still hurt inside.
I still make it out because you love me.

I heal under umbrellas,
In the spring.
I recover with your love for me.
I don't know why you still love me.
Even when I scream at you,
Even when I hide my face.
You are always here for me,
so why do I hurt inside?
Why do I have to hurt?
but I know that in the end,
You will be here for me,
and you always believed in me.

Chapter Twenty
Break Me

Not Likely
Long-Lasting
Sleepless Nights
Uninvited
There?
Try

Will you let me break you down to nothing?

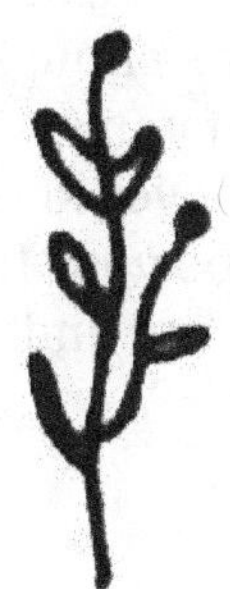

Not Likely

I am not your friend...
It's not likely for me to love you.
I love too hard and that's enough.
I hate myself because of you.
You hurt me in ways I never knew.
It's not likely for me to be your friend anymore
because you created a dead end.

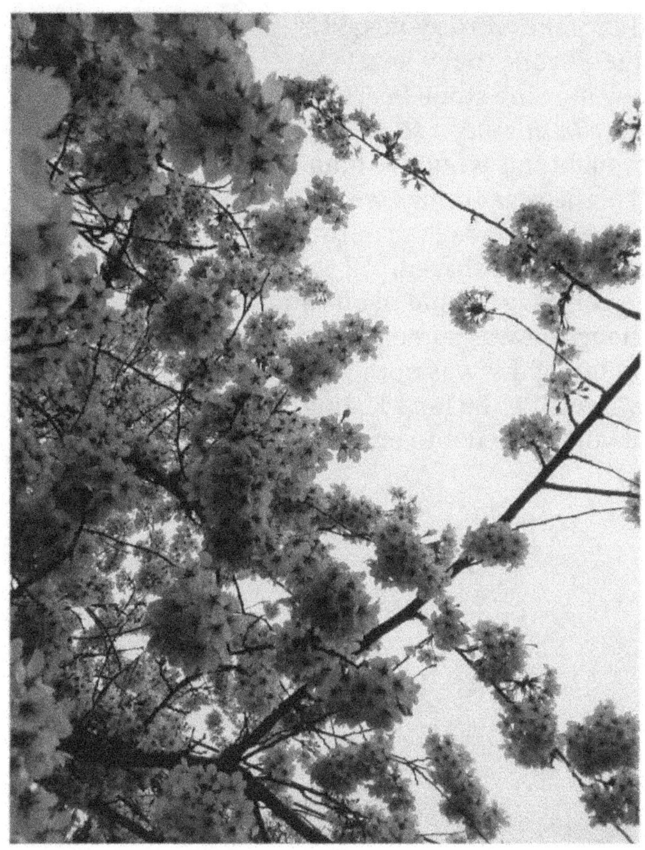

Long-lasting

All the fake words you said
have all gone to my head.
They hurt my stone heart.
How can this mean so much?
I thought this would be long-lasting.
All of the great things we had,
Have all faded back to nothing.
The walks we shared,
The things we found in one another.
I thought it was something,
You thought it was nothing.
I wanted it to be long-lasting
but you wanted it to end in a second.

Sleepless Nights

Let me just sleep on it,
'Cause it is too much today.
I am so sorry for my "issues".
I'm gonna just sleep on it,
if that is Okay.

Uninvited

I’ve been invited to every party.
Nobody ever seems to be sorry.
but I’m fine,
as long as it's okay to be uninvited.
I don't want to join your book club
or
Be involved with your big life.
I’m fine with being uninvited,
as long as nobody cares
if I’m only uninvited.
I can be lonely if nobody cares.
All I really want now is to be alone,
I know that it seems selfish of me,
but I know,
What it's like to be invited
and come over alone.
‘Cause I have run a thousand miles,
and I have never found a better smile.
and I could lose a thousand dreams,
To see your face every morning
because I love you.

You were there since the beginning of my life.
I love how you see me
in the ways, I don't.
You know me better,
Even when I hurt.
So please, let me be uninvited,
From the party of your life.
You always saw me,
Like I see you now.
We're both still cold, and now you're gone.
I am sorry
to say I was wrong.
I have reached love
but nowhere near
the love you gave
because I could be uninvited,
again,
because I miss you
and your being
because it was all here when I was with you.

There?

Be there,
Stay there.
Go there,
Don't go there.
There?
Where is there?
How is it a good idea for you
to not be here
When I have to be there?
Why are you always there?
When I don't need you there?
but when I need you there,
You never are...there
Now these nights I lay alone,
Thinking about how I went wrong
choosing you but maybe I'm wrong.
So look beyond what people say.
I look at actions more than words.
It's always for you.
That's why you're there,
When I don't need you there.
but when I need you there,
You never are.
So when I leave, Remember,
I was always there when you wanted,
Even when I didn't want to be.
I had no freedom or honest love.
That's why I felt alone because
when I was there, you were gone.

Try

I try all the time
to keep it all together
but never had I ever
Stopped trying.
People tell me that I messed up,
Didn't do it right.
My help is never good enough.
I keep trying to fix,
Trying to help,
Trying to make things a little bit better.
If I don't do it right,
I guess I didn't try hard enough.
I never try hard enough.
I try,
I try to help,
Try to fix
but I should stop trying to fix this.
I try because I know that I can't fix me,
so I try to fix things
to make me feel better.
My trying is never good enough,
for anyone.

Chapter Twenty-One
Bluesheets

Object
Black and Yellow
Like Clockwork
Pinkie Promise
How?
Bluesheets
Good Side
Phone
Me
Lovely
Beg
Pictures
Real
Cursed

Would you leave me?

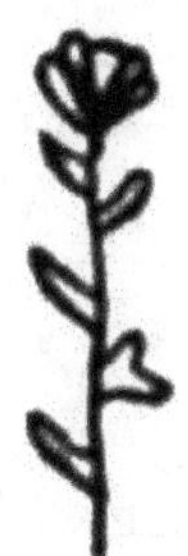

Object

If you're born with it,
You're used for the art.
If you're not,
You have the cards.
soft and sharp
Tissue.
We are all objects.
We never
Played their game right,
The rules burn off the page.
Time catches up
before you turn the page.
They won't watch forever...
You're an object;
Their possession,
and nothing else.
Why don't you understand?
You're not always gonna
be first
because you will
turn to rust,
When they're done
with the object of
your art.

Black and Yellow

Hello from the below,
It's over and all yellow,
Nothing is clear in the darkness.

Like Clockwork

Like one I knew, you had to go.
I never knew it could be so slow.
I knew you had to leave but
like clockwork, it ended me.

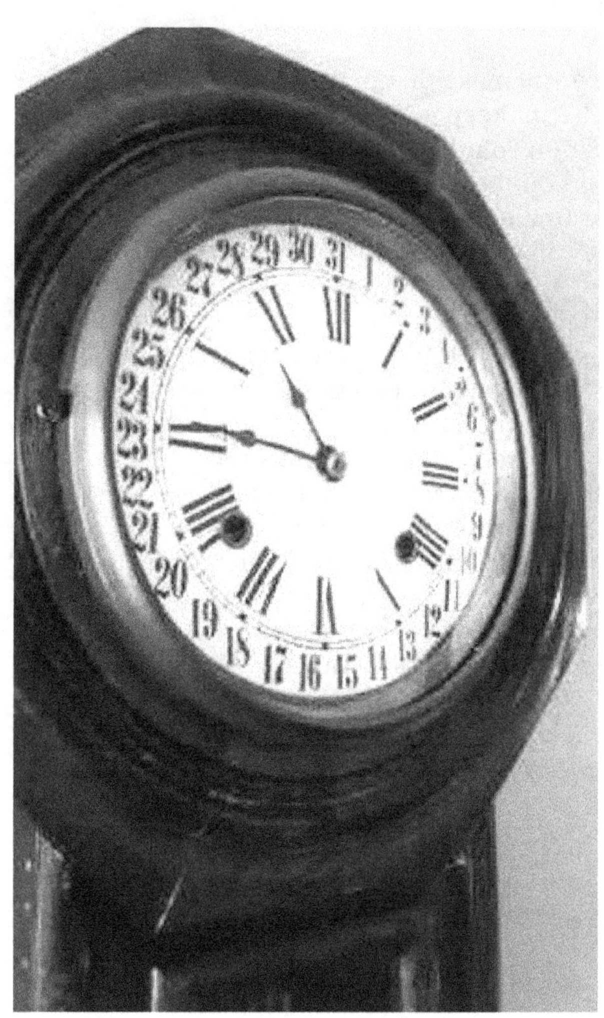

Pinkie Promise

When you make that promise,
You better keep it.
Swear on your life,
Cross your heart,
Hope to die.
That's all you need in a pinkie promise.

You tell me all I know.
You say all the things I already knew.
You promised me everything
but *did I get everything?*
You can't keep a pinkie promise,
No matter what you say to my face.
I keep swearing on it but I never receive it.
You keep walking away from the problems.
I can't understand why
you walk away from this clean.
I know you wanna love me
but if you can't be honest
and keep my pinkie promise.
Then *why should I waste my time?*

I have other people in my life
that I don't regret forgetting.
Being broken hurts so
anything could move me.
Move me.
After you broke my heart,
Broke my dreams,
I stay up most nights
thinking of what I had said to make you go.
When you broke our promise,
You kept walking away.
I am honestly kinda sad you broke our promise and
decided to walk away.

How?

As kids, we learn to grow
but when the sun and moon are taken from you.
How can you grow?
How can I grow with just tap water?
How can I fly with just one wing?
How can I be built to sit alone?
How can one challenge another just to say you are wrong?
How?

Bluesheets

I am caught up in these Bluesheets,
Tangled in them.
Still can't get out of all this trouble.
Can't replace them
With words from my mouth.
These Bluesheets are bad for me.
I still want more, like
Cake and candy,
but it is rotten in my teeth.
These Bluesheets
can't leave me.
The blue follows.
I can't escape,
but I hold onto these Bluesheets.
They follow.
I guess I needed those old Bluesheets
to soak up the pain.

Good Side

On the good side,
We were happy.
We were nothing.
We were happy.
We were nothing.
I was on repeat daily.
You were going through something.
I felt a bridge form,
I knew you fell off.
I held your hand
but then let go.
I was happy.
You were nothing.
I was happy.
You were nothing.
On the good side,
I fell for you.
I let go of you.
I fell for you.
I let go of you.
I fell for... The good side.

Phone

Why am I on the phone?
You're not listening to me.
You don't care about me.
Am I needy?
Am I supposed to care?
Why be on the phone anymore?
Why even care?
Why let go?
Why stay?
Why let go, when I need to fly away?

Me

I am me,
You are you.
I am staying,
You are leaving.
I let go,
You stayed still.
Nobody really knows what you did.
Tell them....

Lovely

Green eyes,
Cursed beauty...
You look lovely.
I would happily give my life for you.
I would change for you,
I will cry for you,
I will beg for you
because I love you.
You're everything I could picture.
You're lovely to me.

Beg

I'm not gonna beg for more
if you can't save yourself for me.
Find someone else, please.
I am not a shoulder to cry on.
I am not a talk to you later.
I will not beg for more
if you can't save yourself time.

Pictures

I was scrolling through my phone
and I found someone.
She was lovely
but hurt me.
I found the picture we took at the vineyards,
She held my hand that evening.
We looked so happy
but *was she happy?*

Real

It's hard to know if we're real,
It's hard to feel anything now.
I knew I was missing out,
When I heard that I may be gone.
I knew the real was far away.
So I stayed up late,
to find a way.
I needed to find myself again.
I was searching and looking,
I could not find myself.
I must be stuck inside
a box with a silver lock.

Cursed

We were hurt from the beginning,
We stood still in the black of night.
I remember holding your hand,
When you told me you felt nothing.
I wanted to let you go
but I didn't want to be the bad guy.
so I waited for you
to say goodbye.
I stood in the daylight,
Daylight where you won't go.
You never said no,
You always nodded the answer.
I should have been smarter,
To know I would fall.
I thought you would let me go,
I thought you left your skeletons...Behind.
How were we cursed from the beginning?
I knew that I wanted us but was I too kind.
Are you blind?
You know I am hurting inside,
I am terrified of what you may do.
You...You ...You...
It was a pleasure meeting you,
but I am done.

Chapter Twenty-Two
Reality

III
Pull the Trigger
When it Gets Hard
Real Life
Hesitation

This is not easy to believe what you see in me

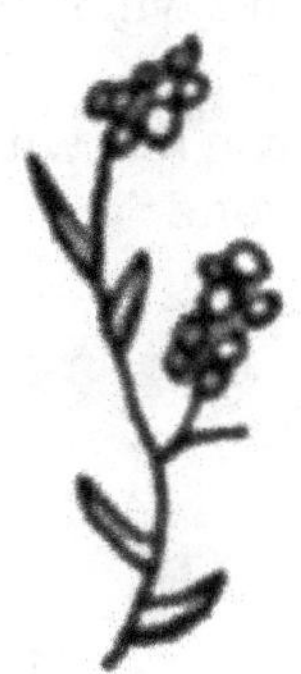

III

I will be alone. . .
I know that it's hard but I will keep walking into darkness.
I will show them they can live without me.
I will show them I am gone
That I am...

Pull the Trigger

You won't shoot.
You won't take the chance
but pull the trigger
and see who you really are.
You're no good guy
but you are no bad guy.
I can't say that you wouldn't before.
You won't shoot now.
You won't do it for me
but pull the trigger.
I bet you'll call help when I drip dry.
Believe me, I don't want to die like this
but if I'm next to you just
pull the trigger.
I might die in more pain,
so do it sooner than later.
I wanna be in your arms
when I die next to you.
I am sick,
so please free me.
Pull the trigger and lay next to me.

When it Gets Hard

Pack up your bags,
Let it all go.
You're done here.
Ready to go.
When it gets hard,
You're always alone.
You can't be freed from the cage.
What do they want from me?
I want someone to care
when it gets hard.
Trouble always follows
when it gets hard.
The danger is near
but I still fear,
When it gets hard.

Moments I Live

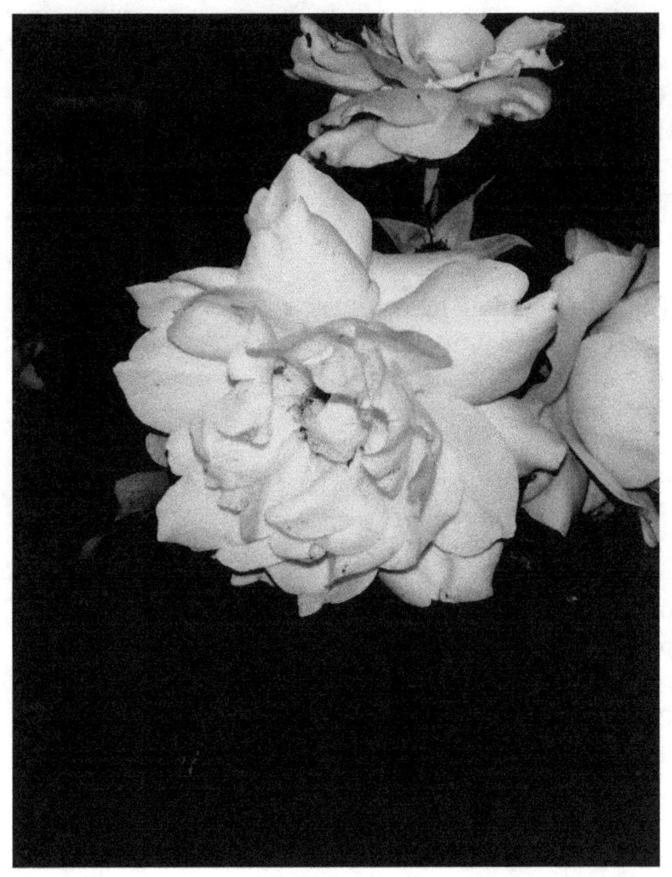

Real Life

In real life
there is sin.
There is starvation.
There is sadness.
In real life,
there is bleeding.
There are broken hearts.
There is brain damage.
In real life,
I'm a loser.
I'm a lost soul.
I'm nobody else,
I'm Me, Myself, and I.
I'm who I am.
I'm real life,
People watch,
People stare,
People hate.
People don't understand
in real life.

Hesitation

Wanting some more
but I can't.
I want you tonight
but I can't.
This hesitation is dark.
Hesitation never leaves
and it gets me in trouble.
Hesitation only pushes my words down to the ground,
it lets cruel hate through the door.
This hesitation is not great.
It never loves,
Never gives...
Only once did I live.
Live in that moment
of being alone.
That is a moment I lived
alone and cried ...for a moment I saw the light
but, then I remembered,
My hesitation owns me.

Chapter Twenty-Three
Chasing butterflies

Don't get lost on your way

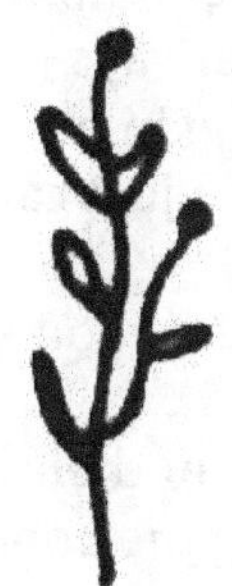

Chasing butterflies

I walked the fields of forever to hold onto the
butterflies but I always end up losing
the good butterfly that always flies away.
I have the flames burning in my eyes and
I can't put them out and I just can't catch the real
thing.
I always end up losing the good kind of butterflies
that always fly away.
I run after the goodness of their light the send to my
chest and I keep chasing the good kind of butterflies.

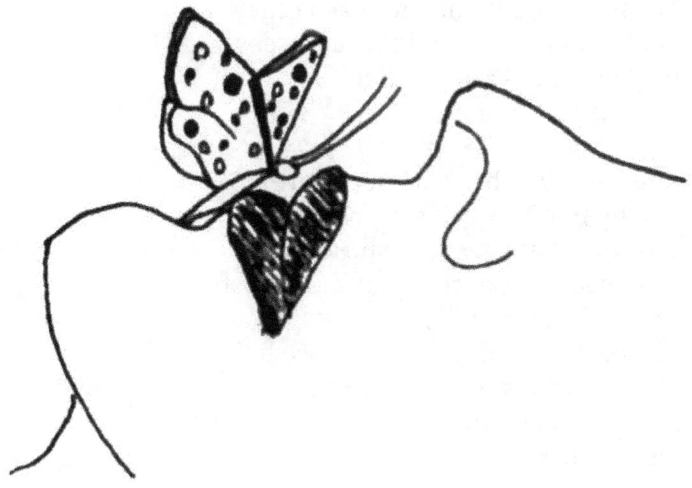

Darkness Sees and Light Does

The dark can see, but
The light completes the painting.
The forces never believe each other
but the light does and the dark sees.
Darkness sees and the light
does…

The dark watches from a picture.
The light follows all the principles.
The forces always fear one another.
They see what each other fears most.
They follow the tale,
The path that they created once before.
The two that were one at a time...
Darkness sees, but
Light does.

The dark is clouded with hate and fear
and the light is broken free of any tears.
Darkness is always in the way of the light of the
future
because darkness sees and light does.

The light does and never frowns.
The dark frowns and never does.
The dark sees from a distance below.
The light falls from a cloud above my head.
The light is in me.
The light is here.
The light leaves its love all here.
The dark gives me fears.
The dark can see my harms.
The dark never wants us to let it go.
The dark sees, and the light does.

We see what the dark does
and we see light looking upon the dark.
The light loves the earth with me.
The dark can see love through my eyes.
I see it all and do it all for me,
so the darkness sees me,
The light shows me,
and the dark and light will never take me.

???

Will it please you,
to paint the black and white on me?
Can I fade to gray?
Can I be the stars without your night?

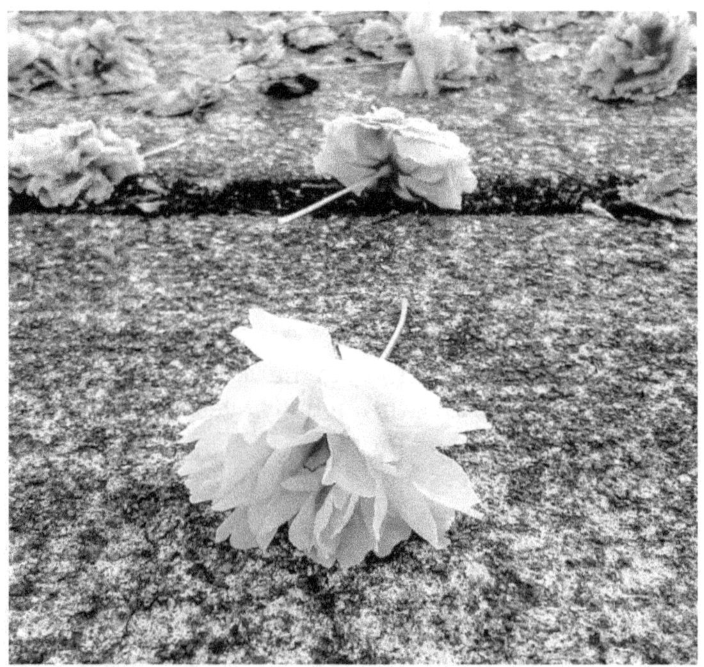

My Rainbows

Red is my bad.
Orange is scar tissue
Yellow is my broken bridges,
Green is the fun I've had,
Blue is my sad days,
Purple is the love I had,
This is my rainbow,
The bits of me no one has,
My rainbow my broken paths,
My rainbow that carries tears,
My rainbow my charm and luck,
My rainbow is what puts me together most days,
My rainbow, My lifeline.

The Storm

As the storm rolls in,
I fall to the concrete.
I wished the sun was here to stay.

Sleeping in Color

Dark dreams of suicide.
Hypnotized to feel this way,
I don't know what else to say.
I may just fall to the sheets again,
I guess you could tell me I've been sleeping in color.

Chapter Twenty-Four
Those Days and Nights

Tomorrow
sometimes
Blue Days
Good
Living
Those Days and Nights

Days go by fast and memories catch up.

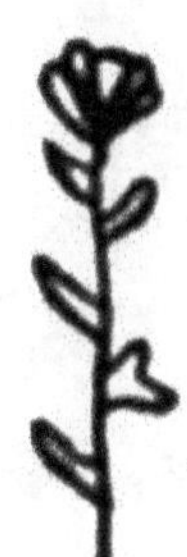

Tomorrow

Tomorrow we live,
Tomorrow we fly,
Tomorrow we trust.
You're just being honest.
Tomorrow we give,
Tomorrow we try,
I'm just by your side.
Tomorrow I love for you,
Tomorrow I live for you.

sometimes

sometimes I tell the truth,
sometimes I give,
sometimes I care,
sometimes I want,
sometimes I love,
sometimes I try,
sometimes I feel sad, but I hold it in.

Blue Days

On these blue days,
I lay alone.
I stay quiet.
I cry alone.
These blue days.

I heard a story about a boy...
He was so blue.
He was unhappy with his face,
so he put himself to sleep.
Now, he's down in history.
We don't know why he did it,
but on these blue days...
On these blue days,
We won't live forever.
On them, we won't survive.
These blue days give take lives.
They break us into glass.
Blue, blue days...
People die.
People cry.
I lay alone
on these blue, blue days.

Good

"You're good."

"but I don't feel good."

"but you're made that way."

Why do they say I'm good?
I don't feel good.
I don't think I'm good.
Am I good?
I don't think I am.
I don't think I'm perfect
but they say I'm good.
I don't think I am, though.
I feel like I'm lost,
Trapped in a loop
of living the dream that wasn't mine.
They keep saying I'm good
and I don't feel that way.
They say I am,
I say I'm not.
They say I'm a good person
but I see a **WORTHLESS** being.
I see a bad person.
I see an ugly person
but they say I'm good.
I don't feel that way.
I don't think I ever will
because I am **not** good.

Living

I live how I can,
I live how I want,
I live the way I think is right
but we are all living and
we all make mistakes.
This sadness and heartbreak is living.
I live to experience.
I live to see.
I live to feel the way I do
but we are all living and
we all have gifts and dreams.
This love and growing is living.
This thunder and anger is living.
I change to live.
I give to forget.
I lose to remember the pain
but we are all living,
We are all giving,
We are...
We, the people, are living.

Those days and nights

Hold me as you used too.
I know you had things to do,
You got sick of me, didn't you?
I didn't mean to hold on,
I hurt you somehow didn't I?
How could you let me go?
I know you wanted to stay
but in the end we still only had...
I'm still trying to figure out what I did wrong,
What did I do to make you leave?
I want you to see how much I changed,
I hope I am not too late for you now.
Those days and nights are all we truly had.
I know I hurt you, I'm sorry.
I am trying to do better
but I wanna know where we went wrong.
I wanna know if all those days and nights,
If they meant anything to you at all.
Can you see that I am new and clean?
I just wanna know where we went wrong.
It won't hurt just to see my face again.

Chapter Twenty- Five
Black Clouds

Not Anybody Else
Just A Breeze
You Know I Fly
Cloudy Day
1000 Stairs
I Can't-Miss You
Lies Are Overflowing
Flooding From Your Tears
Rain is coming
You forget to forgive

Love me like I am already above.

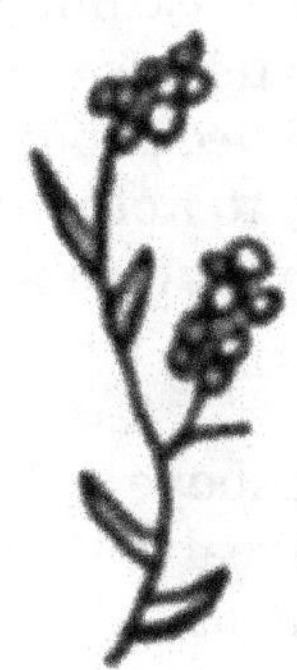

Not Anybody Else

I know I am not happy
but I don't want anyone else but you.
I don't need anyone to tell me what's better for me.
Why is everyone so worried about me?
I don't need anybody to help me.
I can help myself off the bathroom floor.
I know I hurt inside.
I don't want help.
I had the idea of going above
but I know it won't be real if it's a flaw I see.
Why can't I be happy alone?
I can survive on my own
but I will never be happy alone.
Not anybody else will replace
the love I used to have.
Not a soul is as pure enough as heaven above.
How about I go to sleep?
If I sleep? it would help me think.
I still miss the sight of her . . .
Not a person will replace . . .

Just A Breeze

I fly my kite so high,
High enough to touch the sky.
A little wind will lift my spirits.
Just a little push to ease the pain.
You said to feel the pulse of the air,
I know you said you knew but, do you?
Just wanted to ask for help
but I don't know how to ask.
I am just gonna go,l.
I never know how you feel.
Do you feel a storm or a breeze?

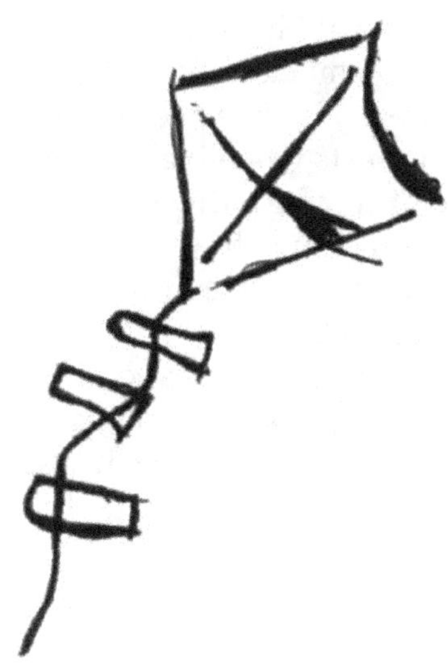

You Know I Fly

"Flying without feathers is not easy;
My wings have no feathers."
~ *Titus Maccius Plautus*

I know you heard I fell
multiple times from the sky.
I know you don't think I have fears
but I hate me for giving off that vibe
because nobody can survive my rain.
I know it hurts when I flee town.
Instead of staying on the ground.
I don't want to stay in that spiral.
I want to stay but if I do I will lose my dream.
I know. I wish that you could come too
and after what I have been through,
There is too much to see in the full
and I hate my hills I have created.
I know it hurts when I fall again,
instead of staying with you.
I know you know I fly.
I know we will get past this.
I want to feel the air.
I want to feel her spirit above.
I can hear her words like bells.
I know you know that I fly away at times.

Cloudy Day

I thought that I knew what I wanted but I forgot in an instant.
You said that you would be here forever
but you lied in my dream.
I can't seem to believe a word you say now.
This cloudy day makes me feel so down.
The weather was so nice and calm.
How could you go to Arvada?
It was so sudden, and I thought you would stay forever...
I guess you knew that you couldn't
Carry me with you on a cloudy day.
Look at you. You're nothing but air now.
I wanted to change for you
and now you aren't here to save me.
I know we had issues.
I thought you would stay, unlike somebody else
but I guess it was my fault for believing the clouds.

1000 Stairs

Every time that you tried,
I walked up to another flight.
I was the one who fell. . .
Fell out of love.
I will try to be safe on my walk up,
I won't jump no matter what.
I left you way too soon to know
and now I regret how I left you.
someone shouldn't leave you,
On another 1000 stairs.

Moments I Live

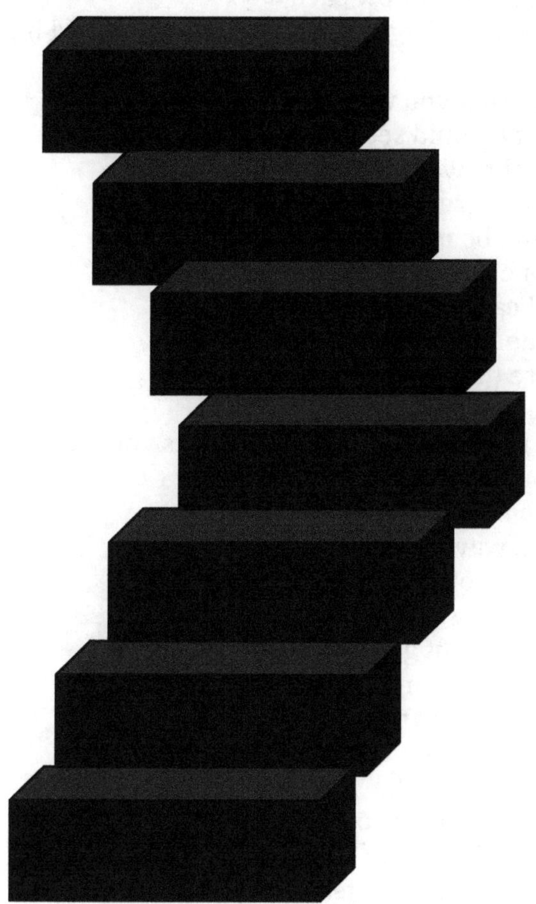

I Can't-Miss You

I look out my window each day.
I can't seem to forget the way you and I would be together.
I thought that you would make it,
I thought I would see you again...
My thoughts were wrong.
I seem to regret not calling again
and I can't be mad at anyone,
it's no one's fault.
I know I can't miss you.
It was too much to lose you.
You were the one that held me up,
The one I miss too much.
I cared, but I never really tried...I was young.

I tried to fix myself
but I was way too young, I felt.
I knew you loved me
but *how am I supposed to feel?*
You left without giving me a warning.
You fell asleep forever.
I can't miss you anymore.
I can't believe you're gone now.
I miss you so much
and you don't have to say a thing.
I knew you loved me
but just like that, you fell asleep
and I have learned something from you,
that I need you.
I can't imagine a life without
our moments of happiness.

I miss you so much,
but I can't miss you now.
I need to move on from this
but it's hard being alone
or feeling so alone.
I just know I can't move on,
knowing you were the one.
Knowing you held me up.
Knowing you loved me,
as I loved you.
I want you to know,
that when I close my eyes,
I think of you guys,
and I cry because I really do miss you guys.

Lies Are Overflowing

Your pain carries disease,
Your heart is so broken.
Your bite is so nice,
Your lies are so frozen.
I knew you were wicked from the beginning.
I knew from the brown eyes that your lies were overflowing,
That you would eventually drown in them,
That you would hurt from the aftermath of the lies,
That you would fall to your knees to the God that you may know,
That you would cry because you told one white lie.

Flooding From Your Tears

I lay upon the mattress downstairs,
Thinking of your hopeful eyes.
You're still upstairs,
Upset and crying about a broken mistake.

How can you say it was from my broken mistakes?
How can you toy with my words?
Is it possible I was the one who made the payment to the devil?

Was it me who took your pure soil away?

The flooding from your tears is haunting me,
and I am just downstairs.
I hear you cry, just like before...
I need the flooding to stop.
I need it to stop before I drown
in my own guilt.
The flooding from your tears must end
before I drown in your tears of pain.
They were the ones I created.
The new beginning for you should be
clear skies now that I am underwater.

Rain is Coming

I can see the clouds above.
They are forming on your behalf.
They seem to possess all of your anger,
Like an angel, you hate your lover
but I fear for myself
that the rain is coming.
The rains of hell
will fall upon my arrival to you.
You seem to hate me.
Then why be with me?
is it the kindness?
is it the eyes?
is it nothing at all, but just to torture me?
is it what you need?
but for I fear
the rain is coming.

You forget to forgive

How do I see the best in you?
Does it hurt you, that you made me cry?
You knew I did the best I could to save you,
I told you that it wasn't possible to live high.
I thought I told you, please,
forgive me.
How am I supposed to not hate me for failing?
You seem to forget to forgive.
I know it hurts you
when I cry every time you tell me
that you didn't love me.
I was being honest
and you broke all our trust into dust.
I hate you for ever needing me to get the dream but,
you always seem to forget to forgive.

Chapter Twenty-Six
What ifs

What ifs
Arachnids
you can tell me
Circus
Does It End?
777
Stay
Ponder
Bury me
burning fields
Afloat
Hot-Air Balloon
Apt. 910
Teary-Eyed
Witness
Wait
I'm ~~Hurting~~
Breathing
Save You
I don't know
I Blame You
Learning Lines
33
Squirt Gun

"What ifs are just questions
created by my broken mind."

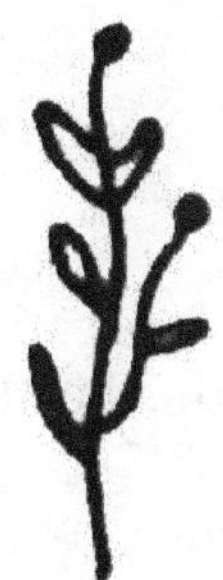

What ifs

What if I die today?
What if I don't make the cut?
What if I'm not successful?
What if I don't impress?
What if I end up alone?
What if I am just no good?
What if I am half of what I breathe?
What if I am nothing to this Earth?
What if I have dark ideas?
What if I don't want to run?
What if she was right?
What if I fall into the romance?
What if I don't have all the good?
What if I am not true?
What if I am not serious enough?
What if the moon falls?
What if I leave too soon?
What if I am a good man?
What if I give up on this plan?
What if I stop and think?
What if I love to thick?
What if I care about you?
What if he lied?
What if I am enough?
What if.....

Arachnids

I heard her scream in the desert;
Falling down her web of lies to eat me alive.
I only ever fall into their webs of disaster,
never do I find love that evolves over time.
My wings damaged from the last love,
I always fall out of a perfect line.
My heart ripped out and replaced with a box of cactus
thorns
arranged in the perfect form.
Arachnids take my heart for the last time.

you can tell me

I know why I didn't try....
I tried to make you want me more than you did.
I just wanted you to know
you can tell me
what I did wrong.

Moments I Live

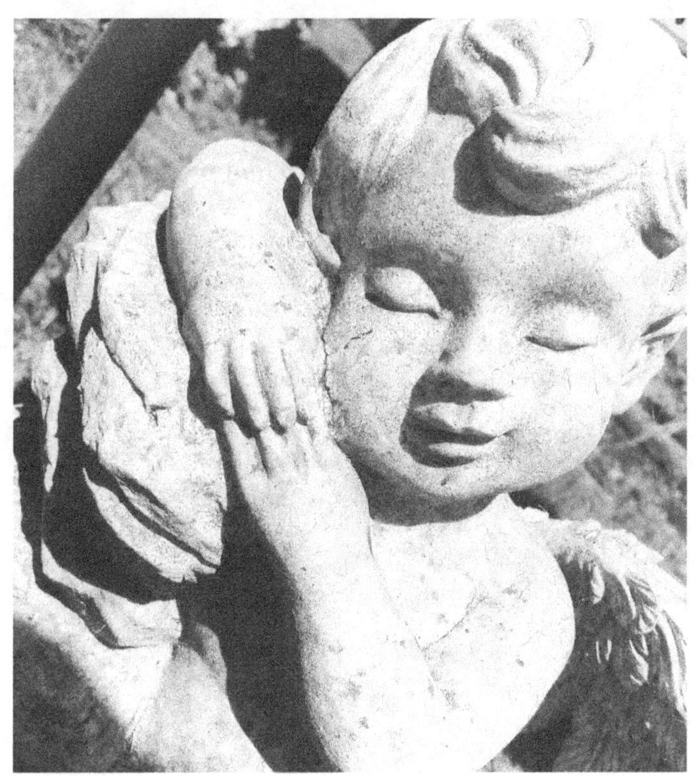

Circus

Fools fall in love with you,
They walk around your circus
to get to your heart of cotton candy.
How do you follow the horse with that pretzel heart?
Your lies always took me by surprise,
When you would be so kind to my face,
such a disgrace to my eyes.
How can your heart handle all of this movement?
My heart can't because it's rusted,
so rotate around his heart instead.

Does It End?

Where will my life stop?
When will I learn?
Does it end?
I have grown so much,
Just in the last 7 months.
I have gone from dark to light
but *where will it end?*

Does it end in death?
Does it end here?
I seek to be the best,
The best that I can be.
I see good for me,
I see good in the ocean of minds.
I see it end with me
but *will it ever truly end?*

777

Every pebble falls to the bottom,
Every night the moon comes back,
Every day the sun rises.
Seven minutes until I go,
Seven hours before the snow,
Seven days end and I know.....
He was here...
He left the flower...
He gave me time...
The time that will fade.
Seven minutes until I fade away,
Seven hours until I gaze into the night,
Seven days before I can rest.
He has come back...
This time with a letter......

stay

stay put.
stay right there.
stay my child.
stay to see the pebble fall.
stay to see the night again.
stay too wake with the sun.
stay so you can say goodbye.
stay before you go.
stay home today.
stay to live tomorrow.
stay to give.
stay because people love you.

Ponder

It's just about 3 am.
A thought just came to mind,
as I sit here and ponder.
Why did you leave, so suddenly?

It confuses me,
I know I was never wrong to you.
I know I would leave me too, if I had too.
I still sit and ponder over the time we had.

I heard you have a new lad,
I hope he gets longer than I had.
I know I would leave me too, if I had too.
It's just a thought...

Bury me

To the ones who knew me,
I love you.
To the ones who hated me,
I love you.
To the ones who were here,
I love you.

I want to apologize for my mistakes,
I tried to be better.
I will be better.
I love you.

Bury me,
Bury the old face.
Bury me,
The old place.
Bury me,
Hide my face.
I love you......

burning fields

please dear creator.
i dont really want to die.
is it really love if she doesnt...
is it pain if nobody broke me?
all i am asking for is put out the fire.
i need pure water to put out the burning
fire.
im looking for.....

every night before i dream.
i pray that i will wake up.
please dear creator.
i do want to live.
all i need is for someone to put it out.

i need to survive.

i am looking for love.

to put out my burning fields.

im looking for strength.

im looking for...

i need love.

i need someone to put out the fire.

someone find me. please.

Afloat

Dreams fade as I walk in the water.
The pale blue sky is whispering
it's goodbye for a few days.
The pond will fill,
and I will sink.

I think to myself,
I can stay afloat just one more day.
I can live with the world above.
As the rain clouds flooded in,
I say one last thing...
Thank You.....

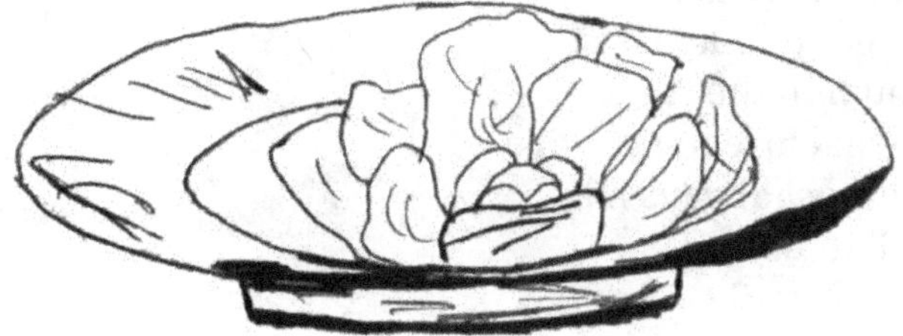

Hot-Air Balloon

You pulled me in
and we were off on
our adventure.
Closer to the sky;
I saw your eyes,
You looked so happy.

Higher we go,
To get to our Oasis.
You pull the ropes,
I lean close to the edge.
I almost always fall...
Fall in Love.

Let's paint the sky,
Just you and I.
From Yellow to Blue,
We were honest and true.
Floating around in the clouds,
I almost always think out loud.

As our peace went on,
A storm began to form.
Once what was you,
is now only Red.
I can only see our relationship
is now forever dead.

Our Hot-Air Balloon,
has been a wonderful distraction.
Your storm rolled in.
I fell asleep
and let you roll out.

I awoke with a clear sky,
brighter than you and I.
I wish the best for our balloon.
I now know it's always good to go home,
Home is where real love lives.

Apt. 910

She always left the light on,
always a new excuse.
I just wanted to be friends,
She never understood what I was saying.
My heart was broken again,
by the girl in Apt. 910.

I loved the idea of friendship
with her.
She finally said goodbye to me,
on her way back to Hawaii.
I gave her a hug and we went our separate ways.
as always I will remember her.

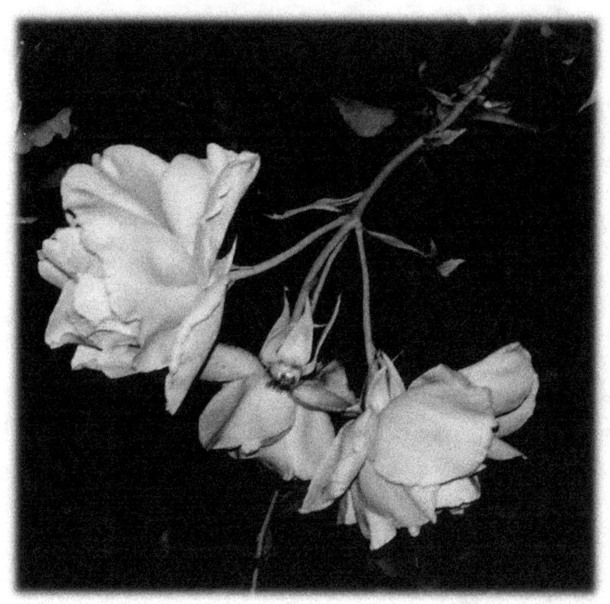

Teary-Eyed

Is medication my remedy
for these tragedies.
My eyes seem to bleed...
this is one of my symptoms.
Does that help you, doctor?

From time to time
my eyes see new things.
Faces.
Colors.
Shapes.
Even though I thought I was alone,
I heard footsteps above.

Is it just me
or are your eyes
black?
Doctor?
Has he taken you away too?
Don't laugh at me,
I'm trying to fix myself.
Don't turn your back
or the tears will possess you.
Doctor, does this help you?
I need to know if you can help me,
Can you cure my dreadful disease?

Give me high doses of antibiotics,
Help me into another dimension.
Stop fooling with my MIND.
Doctor is it just me
or *do you seem to be turning blind?*
My tears seem to just fall,
Fall onto my cheek.
Doctor, Doctor can you help me?
I seem to always be teary-eyed.

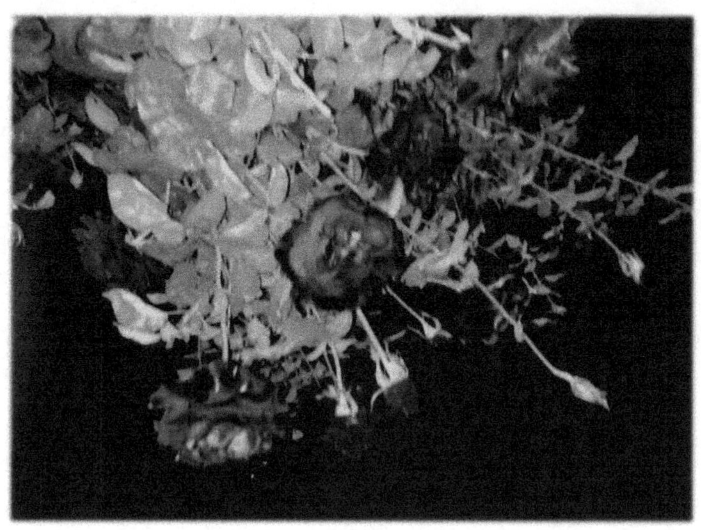

Witness

You want too much from the pond that only carries
small fish.

*Why am I here to witness this mess you still try to
bury?*

I can't wait until you get the diamonds,
Even then you won't be satisfied.
You will swipe your man,
Til debt do you part.

Wait

Cold feet to the broken staircase
and your car is gone again.
I feel nothing warmer than your arms,
You see me alone and then
you still turn away.
Hold me when I have nobody,
When I want you,
When I need you.
I wait for you,
I wait here for you.
I miss your brown eyes
and sweet smile.
How can you turn so bitter?
Did you read my letter?

I wait for your call back.
No text to respond to that,
I can't hold on forever.
I will wait for you;
You never hear my heart calling.
I wait,
I wait for you...
I miss,
I miss you...
I waited for you...

I'm ~~Hurting~~
Breathing

Someone will come into your life and they will take so much of your energy.
I swear the sky falls when we touch;
She may hurt me but I keep breathing.
I know I can make it out
Alive.
Sometimes it's hard to find the one,
She reminds me of someone else I knew before.
How is all of life connected?
She may hurt me but I have to keep breathing.
I know I can make it out
Alive.
I may be out of my mind
but I need to be careful with my heart.
I just have to keep breathing,
Even though I am hurting.
I keep on breathing to release the pain.

She will never understand why it took me so long to get back to her.
I feel my heart pounding,
She keeps asking me the same thing over and over.

Did you ever know me?

I wish I could answer but I have to keep breathing.
You hurt me more than twice and I don't know what else to do so, I just breathe.
I know I am hurting but I have to just keep breathing.

Save You

I told you I was dangerous,
You didn't listen.
forgive me but
I need to save you.
Told you I was hurting,
you broke me down.
I let you go to save you.
Can you forgive me?
I did it for you?
Did I leave to save you?
Carry on without me,
The stars are brighter for you.
I did it to save you,
From the monster in me.
You still ended it all,
You didn't have to go.
I left....it is my fault ...it was all me....can you forgive me?... I am sorry...I try to fix it...I should have stayed.....I left to save you.....I should....I'm...

I don't know

I'm sorry about that,
I said I learned but I lied again.
I don't know what I did?
Do you understand all my doubts?
My fears of losing myself.....
My mind drives down that dark road,
I broke my own headlights...
My face is plastered on your wall and you have to understand I know you're obsessed.

I Blame You

Why do I need to ask them for help?
You should know better than to act on your feelings.
You should know I don't want it.
You should know I wish to be alone in my bed.
You should know I am young.
You should know I am happy.
You should...

Learning Lines

You hang onto the lines from your past.
The lines you have told over the years for the drama club.
You spent hours in your bedroom,
Thinking of ways to humiliate me.
You took the smallest things and turned them into lines of lies,
Learning Lines must feel, *right?*

33

His lighter lit the chemicals,
his cigarette smoke drifts in through my window.
I am here but no one sees how painful it is to be here,
The paint still has to dry on my portrait painting.
I cried to water the wilting flower,
I wanted to scream to you for help...but you seem to shower in his compliments.
How can I live peacefully in your shadow?
How can I dance in yellow, when you paint me in black?

I CAN'T DO IT ALONE!!!

I will wear black scars and the blue blisters for you,
I know I can breathe without you.
I just can't have a life without you.
I need to know, am I value to your life?
Am I talking to air?
It must be all in my head,
The chemicals broke my perfect interior.
I needed to live in yellow
but you painted me black to cover up your white lies.
I wake in the lavender fields made of the day you said goodbye.

Squirt Gun

You were here
and I was there.
Paused in the moment you said goodbye.
I still wait around for you.
I need to move on,
I know...
I still cry alone.
I fill my squirt Gun with all those tears,
That you created for me.
I felt sadness that you'll never know hurt.
I hope you're happy.
I am still hurting
in case you were wondering.
I fill my gun with my fears,
It always kills me that I gave into you.
I fall apart;
very often I doubt again too.
I can't get enough of you,
I might as well leave...
leave it to the hand and gun.

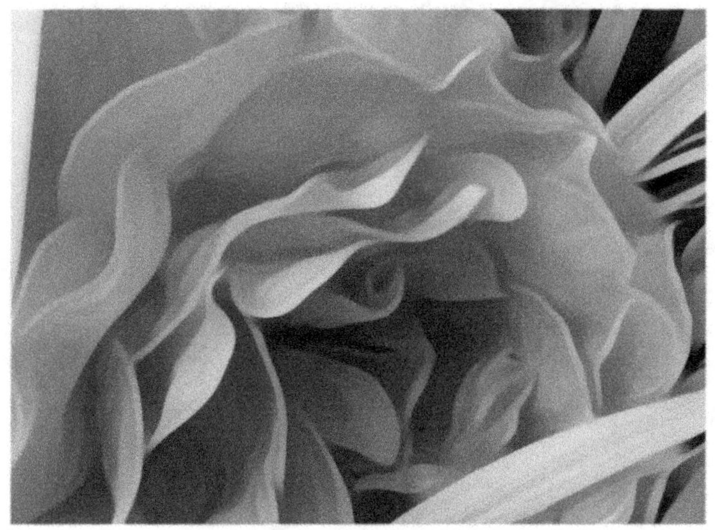

Chapter Twenty-Seven
Raindrops in the Night

Grab your umbrellas

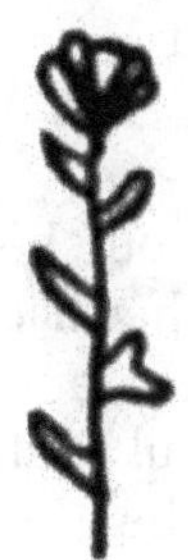

The Dark Fairies Advice

She was always alone.
She only came out at night.
She doesn't understand
why they dislike.
Why they call names.
Why her beauty stands out, before her name.
She doesn't know why her friends are jealous.
She feels isolated, broken, and lost.
She doesn't feel beautiful at all.
She doesn't want to be beautiful,
If she has to feel this way.
She wishes to be ugly
because her beauty is never hidden
and it's all they ever see.
She calls for an answer, but never a response.
Until a tall man asked if she is okay.
She told him no
but the man knew he could make her day.
He said, *"Only true beauty lies within, our world is so thin, they only see half of us, they can't see."*
She knew that to feel loved, you must give love and everyone and everything deserves love.

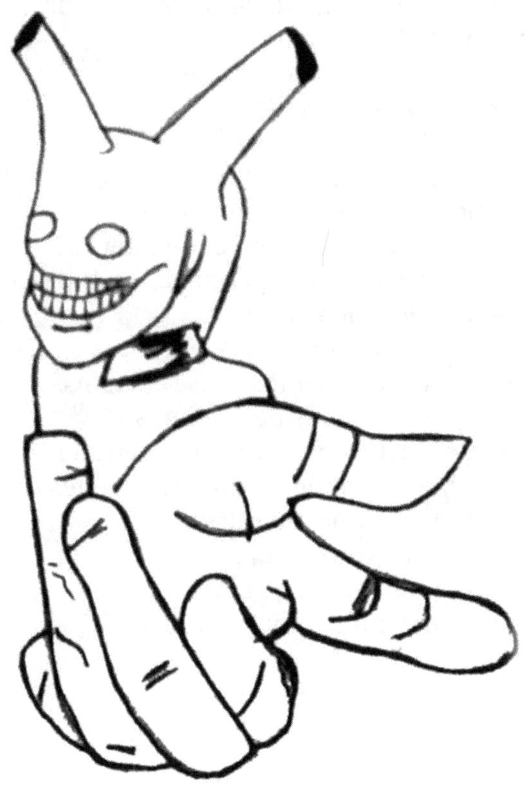

curtains can burn

We cover up the truth with our curtains.
We love to hide reality,
Just don't let them see inside.
My brother gets drunk,
My mom leaves,
My sister gets lost,
and me, never sure who to be.
I close the curtains to hide the interior.
I close these curtains so I can clean the reality.
How will you understand?
You won't, and you don't care.
My reality hides behind these curtains.
I can't give in to this perfectionism.
I cut these curtains so they can see all I see.
I don't hide anymore behind the scenes.
I don't hide my brother drunk,
My mom has gone again,
My sister lost in Michigan,
and me, not sure who I want to be.

I take my match and let go of this and
I watch these curtains burn to the ground.
I watch the truth unravel and
I let these curtains burn down.
The fire takes the reality we put up.
These curtains can't hide you anymore.
I will burn with these curtains to the floor.

The curtains can no longer hide,
My brother asleep under the kitchen sink,
My mom crushed by the broken men,
My sister left in the woods to her death,
and I burned alive with the last breath.

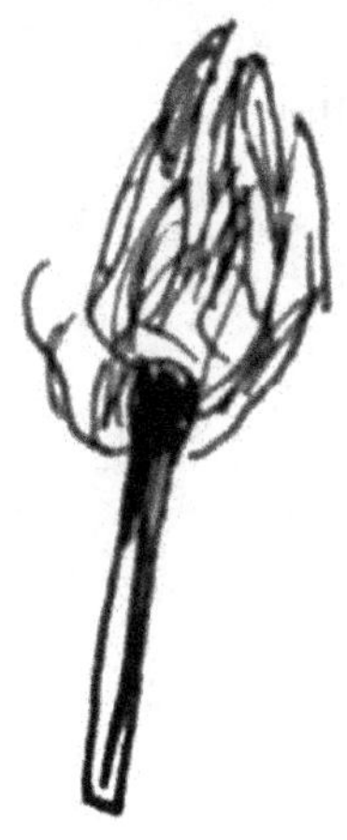

Raindrops in the night

I know you don't want me in your arms.
I just wanna tell you one thing,
Look at all the umbrellas, in the sky,
Envision us up in the clouds above.
I just want to hold you in the storms,
in the sun and clouds holding on.
I know life doesn't hand you what you want;
I do wish that you would stay.
Hear me when I say I love you,
Cause I do.
You were so close to the cliff,
I picked you up and flew away from this.
Hold onto me.
I am staying,
No more running on two feet.
Stand under my umbrella,
I will hold you through the cold
raindrops in the night.

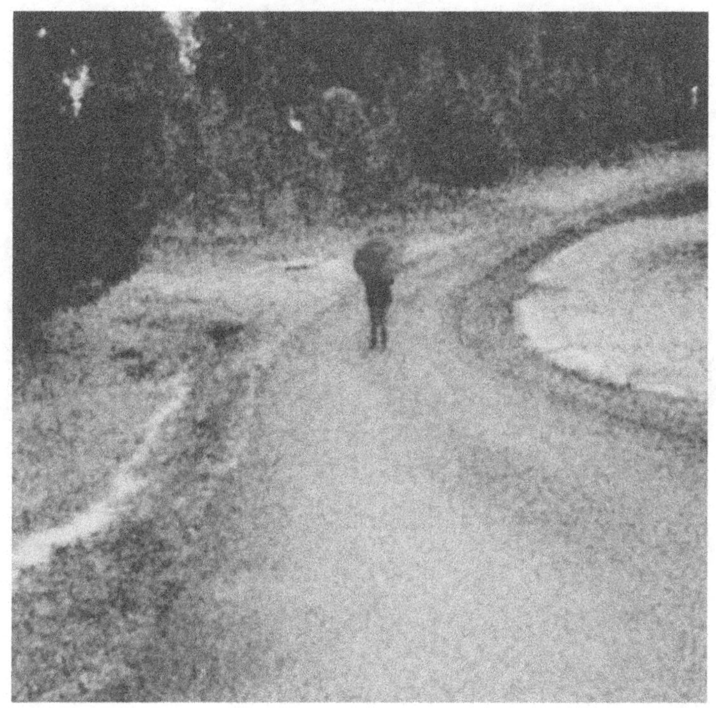

cry sometimes

Sometimes, I can't be right, but I cry sometimes to
live out of this trap.
I cry to find love,
I cry when the stars are out,
I cry to the moon...
I cry sometimes.
I cry for a purpose and for nothing.
I cry for being untrue,
I can't be good for everyone.
I cry sometimes,
That's being honest.
I cry for control.
I cry for help.
I cry for something I can't have.
I cry for you,
I cry for the pain to go away.
I can't always have what I want but I cry sometimes.

Night Light

You can be my night light.
Protect me from the darkness.
You can hold me close when there is no hope.
You can be my blanket to keep me warm.
When I need a night light, you're here.
You always care,
You always love,
You always know just what to say.
You always believe in me.
You are honest in many ways.
You can always be my night light.
Keep me away from the villains in this story.
You can,
You will.
You will care.
You will love.
You will know what to say.
You will be honest.
You will be here for me.
You will always come first.
You will be my only night light,
that I hold onto.

Mooncrows

They travel like Mooncrows.
They attack like vultures.
They don't run and hide.
They don't just follow,
They hunt you down.
Those Mooncrows are demons from the sky.

Those tales of angels above
Say it all about those Mooncrows.
They fly, they cry, they love...
Those Mooncrows wanted to die.
They want to be mistreated,
They wanted hell unleashed on them.
Those Mooncrows didn't care about the moonlight.

They don't wait for the moon;
They wait for you.
They hide, they mourn, they hunt
but why listen to this?
but why is the reason?

When you're a toxic person,
You're a **Mooncrow**.
They will hunt me now.

Sharing is Caring

Why care and never share?
Give me a reason.
This is not fair.
I wish you the best,
Even if you don't
but I wish
that you would give a little,
Not just take it all.
You never care.
You never share.
Caring for me is sharing
but you don't care.
Give me a reason.
No, You don't want me.
No, You don't want us.
No, You never commit.
We know sharing is caring
but you don't share.
So *why should I stay*
If I can't have you
the way I want you?
I guess I'm running,
I guess I'm flying,
I will remember this toxicity
and the fact that
you never shared or even cared.

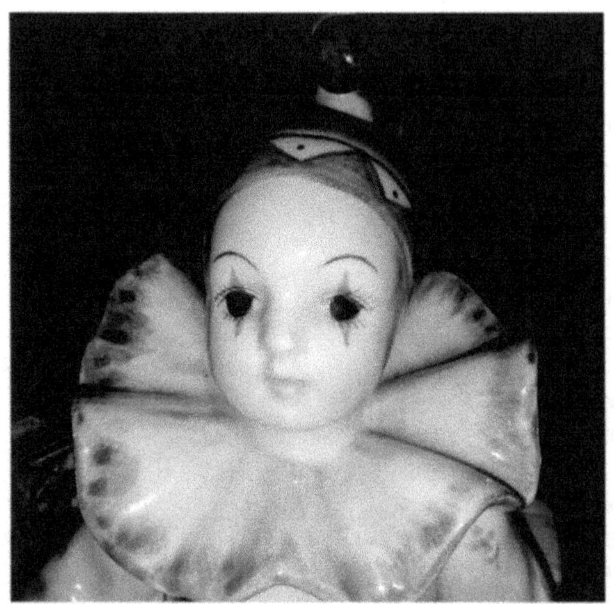

Midnight Mime

Nighttime ghosts;
My soul outside.
The Midnight Mime watches in silence,
Shows my path in silence.
The black night was in silence.
No car sounds,
No birds chirping,
Just the Midnight Mime in *silence.*
He shows me the way.
He cares about me.
The Midnight Mime lives in the night.
He dances with clowns.
He flies with crows.
The Midnight Mime has a purpose in the night.
He has a reason to take my soul.
He watched in silence.
He never comes out in the daylight,
but then it hits midnight
and the Midnight Mime watches again.

Raindrops

They fall from heaven.
Those raindrops gave me light,
They gave me love,
They even made me cry
but they gave me those raindrops,
These raindrops are from above.
They fill the world with love,
for me, these raindrops are heavenly.

They show me the good in what we had.
These raindrops are an angel's cry.
They cry...
but they give us light.
They give us happiness.
They gave us what we have.
These raindrops mean you were heavenly.
These raindrops fell
from heaven and holy light.

Delphiniums

How do I know you love me,
When you never show up?
How do you feel, when I give up?
Petals from your flowers,
Wilted in the sun.
You never gave them love,
Then they dried up.
How do I feel your presence,
When you're nowhere near?
How do I live without you here?
Why do you say you can,
When you know you can't?
Why am I asking questions?
You will never answer them,
You never answer me.

Every Time I was with you,
I felt haunted by a ghost.
Everywhere we went
You left me with a scar
Every time you broke my heart,
You'd cover the mark
With a Band-Aid.
I know you have a good heart
but *why do you fall apart?*
When I get close to the real you?
When I find out the truth?

It's not that I don't love you anymore
but you put the blame on me
You handed me the shovel
and told me to forget
but I can't forget we buried lies to thrive.
I wanted you to be happy,
Why are you upset?
I am sorry that I couldn't save you from yourself.
I'm sorry that I gave up on you when you left me for
the man in blue.

Every Time I was with you,
I felt haunted by a ghost.
Everywhere we went
You left me with a scar
Every time you broke my heart,
You'd cover the mark
With a Band-Aid.
I know you have a good heart
but *why do you fall apart?*
When I get close to the real you?
When I out find the truth?

I can't be around to please you anymore
so I am going to walk away before I break into butterflies.
I left you with the sunflowers yellow and the delphinium too.
I broke my heart so you wouldn't be blue but that didn't matter much to you when I chose to walk away because you chose another, and I wasn't going to wait for a ghost.
I now carry around my band-aid heart because I haven't been the same since we broke apart.
I hope you remember the last days we had because they were bitter like you and
The flowers never grew back in June
but your heart finally turned black.
I remember that I loved you
but I left because you never made me feel special.
I watered your roses,
but You didn't notice.
You just waited
and waited for them to die.

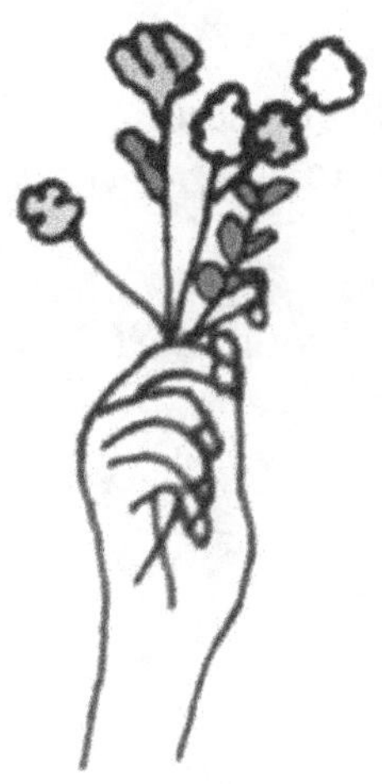

Love Me

Can't you just love me?
Can you give me time?
Can you take from me?
Can you make me feel alive?
Can you give me what I want?
Can you just love me?
Fake it if you have to.
I just want your love.
Just want your body and soul,
Just want to be next to you,
Want to be with you,
Want you to love me,
Want you to give me your heart.
Can't you just love me?

Yes.

Live a Little

Live a little to be free,
Live a little to be you,
Live a little to have fun,
Live a little to create,
Live a little to give hope,
Live a little to begin your path,
Live a little to have some regrets,
Live a little to be who you are,
Live a little more.
I live a little just to be me.

Chapter Twenty-Eight
M

Intro - Blue Feather
Unpredictable Four
The Tree
Glass Vase
Straw Hat
River of You
Goodbye for Now
Ray of Sunshine
Library of the Mind

Turn out the life in someone's eyes,
It can really break a person inside.

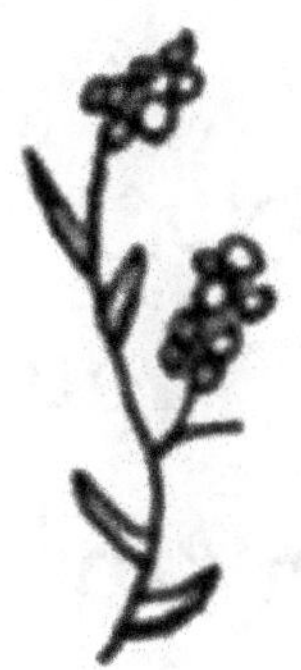

Intro-Blue Feather

Here's a feather
It is blue
To let you know
We remember you

I see the writing on the page.
I hear your words and thoughts go
through my brain.
I see that you wrote, You remember me
but *how do I say I remember you?*

Unpredictable Four

Used to be alone without you all.
Never did I think, you'd be my friend at all.
Pretending everything was all right until then was how I kept going on.
Remember that it's the just four of us,
Even if we end up moving apart.
Divided we might be but it will always be the four of us holding one together because that's what I remember being when we were the unpredictable four.
I want you all to be happy.
Can we all promise to try and
Trust that the end of a call won't be goodbye.
All of us will remember to be forever the unpredictable four because that's who we are together.
Believe in one another and
Listen to everyone because we all want what's best for you.
Even if we end up moving on this.
forever I will remember us and
Our story will be written down.
Unpredictable we maybe but
Remember we are just four human beings trying to see the world around us.

The Tree

A little tree,
She was.
She grew to be so tall.
All the time she spent **Wondering** what she was to do at all.
Years passed and she kept **growing**.
Then one day she fell,
The people cut her down and used her branches.
She didn't know what she did wrong.
Her heart was torn in different places.
She was here and there. . .
The tree was now the home for many,
The tree that was so tall, has helped so many.
The tree that fell.
Now knew what her purpose was,
She was to help us all.
The tree was to hold all of us in full color.

Glass Vase

Little birds sing their tune. . .
She sings with them too.
She walks the road of a strong woman,
She holds people up to where they can grow.
She has held me up to the clouds. . .
Till I was ready to fly.
The glass vase held her flower.
Wilted once and then reborn,
Like the way, she helped us soar.

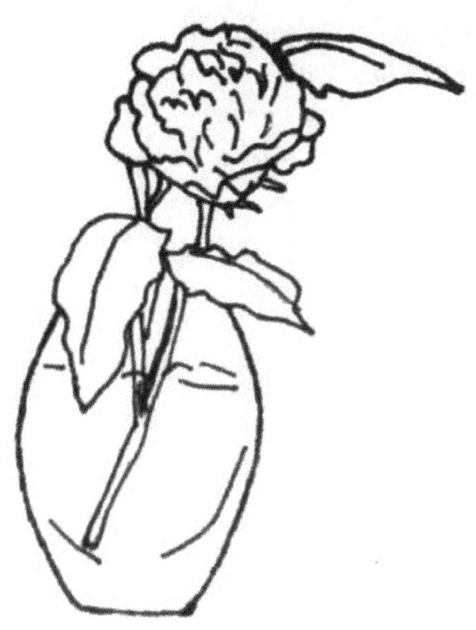

Straw Hat

He held me on his shoulders,
so I could be tall like him.
He held me close through the storms that rolled in.
He taught me to love others,
Even if they had sinned.
He used to wear his straw hat
Outback.
Till one day I wasn't there when a big Storm came in.
He was nowhere to be found. . .
I looked high and low,
He was gone. . .
His straw hat lives outback and
now he lives in my heart.

River of You

You walk me down to the river.
Where we sit and fish together.
You help me reel in the catch
because I am younger then you are wise.

I think I would cry if I ever have to go
to the river alone.
I think I would be all right to say goodbye but
I'm not there yet.
You can't go away to the river of you.
It would make me so blue.

You walk me down to the river
and we talk forever.
I'd catch 1, you'd catch 9.
That's truly no surprise
that you'd blow
my mind.
because you are kind to the river.

I think I would cry if I ever have to go
to the river alone.
I think I would be all right to say goodbye but
I'm not there yet.
You can't go away to the river of you.
It would make me so blue.

Goodbye for Now

How do I say it the easy way?
I don't know what to tell you, what do I do?
I lost someone that felt new.
I could drive up and down a hill a thousand times,
I could cry to every ballad about life,
How is it this easy to lose someone you loved?
I know it's life but, why does life have to suck so much?
I could cry, I could be angry but, all I feel like doing is feeling nothing.
I miss you already and I can only hope I'm ready for the battles ahead of this grief.
I know you've flown away.

How do you lose someone who hasn't told you goodbye?
How can you miss someone when they never called?
How do you love someone you barely see?
I don't know but I saw his soul through the voice on the phone when he knew he had to leave the only thing he's ever seen.
I can't be wise right now.... everything is cluttered with the sound of "I'm sorry for you" but I can't help you.

I will miss you.
I will love you.
I will remember you.

All I know is that it helps to hold onto your soul while I find the rest of mine, now that you're gone away for a long long time.
I want to thank you for being a father who let me be me before I knew who I was.
I want to love you but now you're farther away, so it's much harder to say I love you that way.
All I know is that it helps to write to you this way, and for tonight I'm gonna say goodbye for now.

Ray of Sunshine

She used to walk the sandy beaches
but now she lives in his garden.
She loved the sunshine,
She loved the things that it brought to life. . .
She loved everything about the Earth.

She held me so close,
That when she was gone, I was devastated. . .
She was gone like the sun,
The clouds of a storm wiped out her light.
She flew up high to be with him.
Her Ray of sunshine still lives here,
My storms have disappeared.
How can she leave me all alone?

I cry,
I break.
I miss her to this day,
She is gone and there are so many things I would like to say. . .
I loved her,
I didn't want to see her go. . .
She still shines above though.
Every day when the sun comes out,
She comes to see me live as she did before. . .

Library of the Mind

Walking along the rows of columns of all the past
hardships I had to get through
to the now.
I can see how I was mistreated
and I can't have that now.
I am going to never settle for less than I deserve
cause I deserve the love I give to myself first.
The library of the mind shows me that I deserve to
have the greatest love.

Chapter Twenty-Nine
Immortal

To live feeling free is to become immortal.

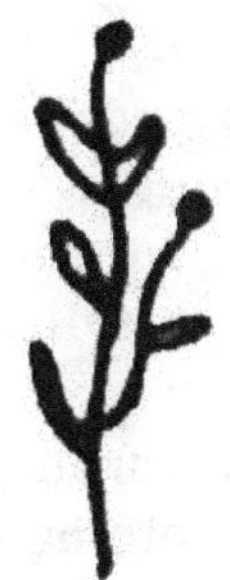

Introduction .
Tape Measure

Does it take a lot of love
for me to satisfy you?
It's hard to count what I gave.
Does it take a tape measure
to measure our love,
or does it take a break
to fix you up?
because I am six feet away from you.
You're above, and I feel nothing still.
Did it take a tape measure
to measure our love?

Mortal

I'm human,
I know.
I love,
I cry,
I even try to fix things.
Is it ever good enough?
Is it how I am supposed to live?
No, but I'm only mortal.
I don't have any superpowers,
I am not any superman,
I am not an immortal,
I'm only mortal.
I'm only half of an angel,
I'm only strong sometimes,
I'm only lonely because I thought
no one loved me,
I'm only mortal.
I can only give so much.
I can only love so much.
I'm only mortal.
I am only me
and me alone.
Just accept we are all human.

The Man in Power

How can I **see it through your eyes?**
I don't understand why it has to be this way
....could you **explain it to me?**

If the man in power wasn't so cruel
I would love Myself
but **I don't.**
If I was the man in power,
maybe **I would think differently**
about all the hours
I spend waiting for me
to love me.

If I was the man in power I would say
the world isn't black and white
its full of color
....how can you of all people not see that
....I want to love myself but
the other part of me hates what I see...
It hates everything about me.

Try Harder

You say you love me;
You need to earn that.
You need to try harder.
Do you want me?
Try to keep me.
I am not your game.
There is no win or lose.
You say I want your love,
I say try harder.
My love isn't hard to find,
You just have to look.
You just need to get close.
I say try harder with every move.
My life is forever with you
but my love is not.
so if you want me,
You need to try harder.
You got to,
You have to.
if you want me,
Try harder.
Try to love me the right way.

Golden soldier

I hate wars.
I see them start in her eyes.
I am ready for every battle
with my sword of strength.
I won't bow.
I wish I was a golden soldier...
I can fight it.
I will conquer her love.
I will take the kingdom, always
like a lion,
They will hear me roar in the night.
Like this shield
my heart is protected by its life.
I am stronger than I was after the battle.
It hurts when you keep those soft apologies.
I won't give up, because I am a golden soldier.
I will bring you to justice,
You have been warned.
I left my sword at your knees,
So please, let me be.

The Final Act

The final act is in between the curtains.
The final act has just begun.
The final act has never happened.
The final act is unwritten so far.
The final act is never-ending.
Why must the act end?
This act is phenomenal
but all classics come to an end.
Like she was put to bed,
Like storms that happened before.
The final act is going to be a blast.
The final act is a pool of tears.
Please, don't cry, it isn't over
but there is no sequel.
The final act, it ends in a while.
The final act will be the death of the soldier.

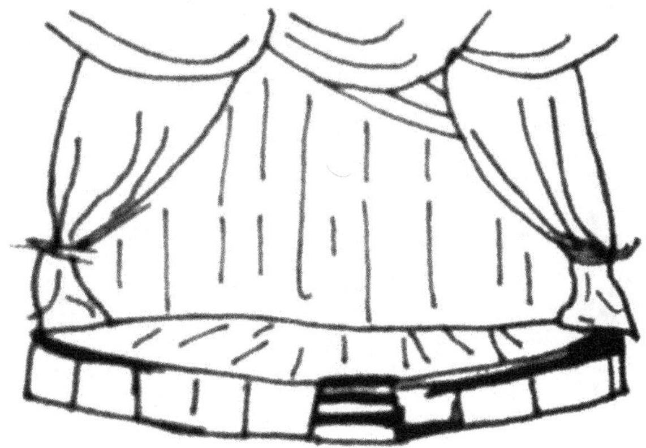

Chapter Thirty
I'm Still Sane

Sane
Everywhere
Arizona
Selfish Love
Feel Me There
Insane

Carve my name into the canyon.

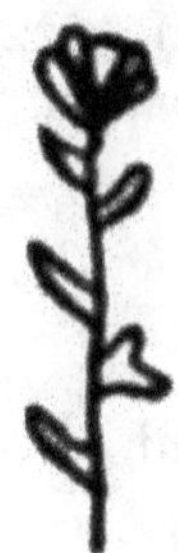

Sane

How can I keep it to myself?
I don't know how to help.
I wonder what makes me crazy...
I live in my own imagination,
I write my own sanity,
in place
of reality;
Of my sanity
... I keep running around,
Talking out loud,
Jumping in the air,
I honestly just don’t care.
So give me some of that sanity.
I am not insane
but I am not tame.
Don't find me.
I won't find you
because I am sane.
Don't you agree?

Everywhere

I still see her everywhere,
In every face I see.
Only I want to feel her here.
I still want her all the time
but she will never be mine
and I still see her everywhere,
in all that I see...
but she doesn't belong to me,
or anything I see.
Everywhere I look,
Everything I touch;
I sense her everywhere.
I feel it, like, all the time.
She is everywhere in my mind.
Everywhere I look, I see her face.
I see her laugh at me.
I still see her, though.
Never will I hide anywhere
from her being everywhere.

Arizona

Red burning in the sky
like Saturn in the night.
Your eyes like fire,
Your soul like sunshine...
You're like Arizona.
I only wanna be loved,
so please, don't hurt me, love...
Red burns in your soul,
So that shadows can't overflow.
Cactus green shines bright
in your eyes.
Coyotes running with the wind of the night
and you tell me it will always be this way.
When I can't say goodbye you tell me, that I will be
your Arizona as long as you live.

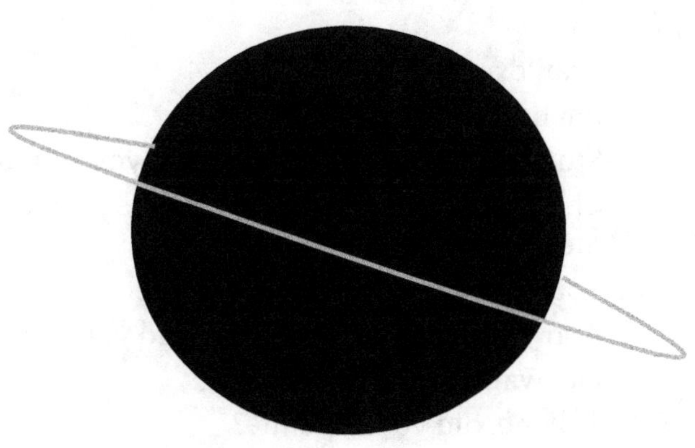

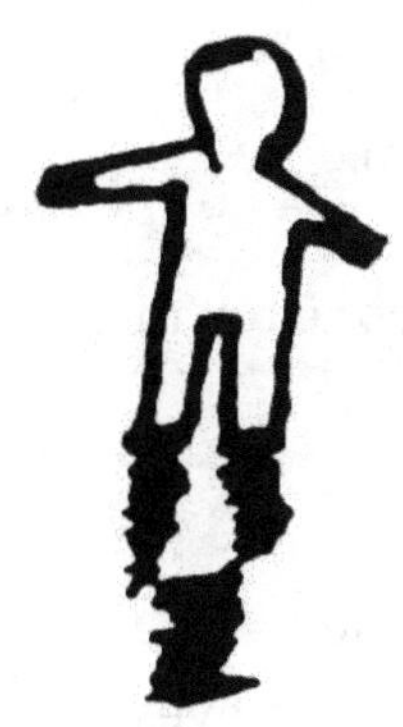

Selfish Love

I can't see us now,
I'm brokenhearted
Stuck on the tennis court where you dumped me.
The blame you put on me over the phone is pushing me down.
You still don't know who you are
And you say I'm the one who did you wrong
all i wanna is the truth
Tell me, did you lie to me?
Leave if you're done with me
But at least now I know.
it wasn't loving me,
It was always loving him.
Cause all you ever do
is love yourself and anyone but me.

You don't love me,
You only love you.
You handed me selfish love.
You told me with red in your eyes that you loved me.
But you don't.

I wasted my time, my energy, and headspace.
You only ever worried about it if I found out.
You can keep your lover...and choose to walk away.
I still feel betrayed
but at least now I know.
it wasn't loving me,
it was always loving him.
All you ever do
is love yourself and anyone but me.

You don't love me,
You only love you.
You handed me selfish love.
You told me with red in your eyes that you loved me.
But you don't.

Your love is selfish
I guess i was clueless
I Mistook it for real love,
I thought it was something i could rely on
but at least now I know.
it wasn't loving me,
it was always loving the him.

you never loved me,
now I'm broken.

Feel Me There

I want you to feel cold
like when you turned your back.
I don't love you anymore.
I'm not taking you back.
I want you to feel me
when you leave.
I will never give it up.
I know I am there.
I want me there when you go.
and all it takes is blaming me for your break-up in the past.
Don't say I haven't warned you.
You know I want you to feel me there.
I want you to feel #blessed.
I let you go.
That's not easy for me.
I love too hard,
I want you to feel loving.
I want you to feel me there.
I love the way you move,
so I want to be there.
I am there in your arms.
I guess I am feeling now,
I am Not your lover.
I am an old feeling
that you still feel within your bones.

Insane

You know you make me feel
What I don't feel alone.
I feel your waves that make me insane.
I have expectations for you.
I don't ask for much, but when I do,
I like you there insane with me.
I like you anywhere but with them.
Don't call me out on my honesty.
Don't respect. Well,
I guess I lost,
because you drive me
insane sometimes.
I don't know who to be,
I don't know what to say,
because you make me
go insane sometimes.
but I don't have a choice.
You know,
You know that I couldn't fall,
When you,
When you...
I feel you around me in the dark.
I shouldn't keep you in my heart
but I call for you.
You never call me back
but you make me go insane,
You only make me go insane, sometimes.

Chapter Thirty-One
Love-Less

Love Blind
No Flores
End Here
Golden One
Psychotic
You
Me and I are no Longer Together

Can anybody really love me anymore?

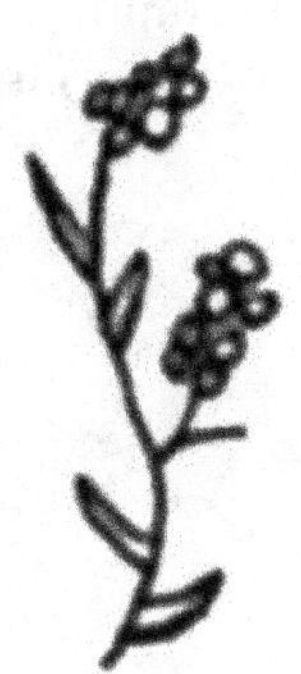

Love Blind

They say that I'm too
love blind to even understand.
When, in reality, I knew it was clear to see
That I was love blind
and I am so clueless
when it comes to love
because I love blind.

No Flores

I haven't received a flor
but I have seen others receive tons of flores
but there are no flores for me.
No flor for me to keep.
No love to give to anyone else.
No love to get from anyone else
but I see all my friends receive flores
and it seems so unfair
but I wish that I could also receive a flor from
someone.

End Here

How can I end here?
Why am I in so much fear?
How do I escape this path?
It's okay, just relax.
I will end right here,
Even when you're not here,
All I know is,
I can't lose my sense of self around you.
All you do is hurt me,
you break my heart in two.
I never knew it could have been you.
I'm gonna end here
and it's okay to say that it wasn't you.
It wasn't me.
It was us as us.
Now I'm stuck, so end here.
Thanks for the help getting up.
I felt my pain as I fell frontwards,
I hit my knees on the bare sidewalk.
I know, I tried, and I tried, and I tried
but it will never be enough.
So I'm gonna end right here.
You have to learn, to let me go
but we could end right here....
That's all I really know.
How can I end here?
How do you end there?
I can't be loved by you,
so I will end it here before you end me.

Golden One

Used to feel like I didn't deserve you.
Used to feel like I had to prove something.
Used to feel like you didn't trust me.
Wanted us to be so much more.
I used to let some people tell me what you were but
now I don't care what they say
because you're my **golden** one.
You are so full in my heart.
You held me to the broken art until you too fell apart
like gold melted to the saddest form.
You used to be my **golden** one before you ran.

Psychotic

How can I be this?
When you're that?
Label me with those stickers.
Call me names that I do not wear.
I guess calling me psychotic,
makes you feel better.
It doesn't hurt you
like it hurts me.
Now, in the back of my mind,
I hear you screaming
but *what the hell do I know?*
What do I know
about how to feel?
All I see is that you're evil with your words.
I guess I am too if you label me with terms.
so I guess calling me psychotic
is something you can do
to make yourself better.
How about I call you out?
Does it make me better?
Am I better than you?

Do others make fun of you
like you make fun of me?
I guess calling me psychotic,
Makes you better, but worsens my self
but whatever works for you...
Call me name after name,
Even though you don't know who I really am.
Dear friend, call me names,
That I will never wear on my chest.
Call me things you think I wear the best.
I may be psychotic in your head.
I hope one day you can get this out, then.
Old friend, *why are you cruel?*
I guess I am psychotic, according to you.
but *what the hell do I know?*
I guess I do know now.
You call me things those kids called you
and I guess you have heart, but it's empty too.
I thought I had a friend,
I guess they were buried
six feet underground,
I knew you were hurt but I never knew this.
Oh, friend, h*ow can you be so cruel?*
I guess call me psychotic,
so I can mean that much to you.

You

I could be wiser.
Your lies were a bit stronger.
You're just as I remember.
You're smile still gets me, through it all
and I am never sure who started the war
but I remember that it was you running.
I'm sure it was you
because after all, I did,
You still wanna hurt me
and now your leaving
with all my pieces of me.
I know it's not likely for me to love now
but I considered your feelings
because after that storm you created,
I'm kind of done with this.
You know it wasn't me starting the war.
It sounds like you promised too much.
Do you want to run or stay?
In a second, you came back to my mind.
I still feel it all but you know you don't at all.
It was just like you said: *I'm gone.*
I never told anyone;
Not even you that I fell in love.

Me and I are no Longer Together

I don't fit with me,
I don't fit with him.
I seem to fade to the background a lot,
I fall each time I see myself better,
That's why me and I are no longer together.
I can't be with something I am not,
I can't fit into that neighborhood.
I am me and he is I.

Chapter Thirty-Two
Blue People

Labels *don't define people.*

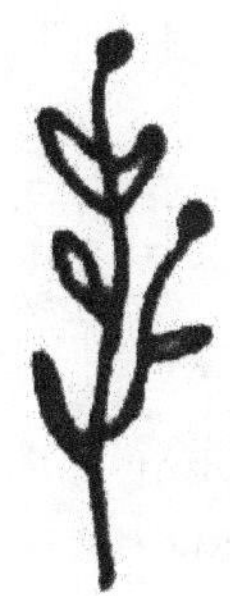

Introduction .
Live One Valued Event

If I lived today,
I would call for you.
So I could tell you.
I lived one valued event
and that I was loved.
I know you miss me
but life isn't fair to us.
If you live one valued event,
You will be forever loved.

Dancing on Water

I feel like breathing is harder,
Then it used to be.
I feel like swimming in the ocean,
Float me down a river,
To get to her.
Tell me where she goes.
To dance on water would be a dream,
If only she were here with me.
To dance on water with her,
Would help me drown out the pain.
To dance on water.....with her.

Standstill

End your tears,
Stop them right here.
The train is moving on to the stop where we move on.
It is beautiful that you even exist at all,
Your tears flow one by one,
to the river where you standstill.

Papers of your heart burned away
by his fire eyes,
End your fear,
Stop fighting here.
The train is moving to the next stop where we move on.
It is beautiful that we exist in this world we call home.
Your fears float away one by one,
to the forest where you standstill.

Moments I Live

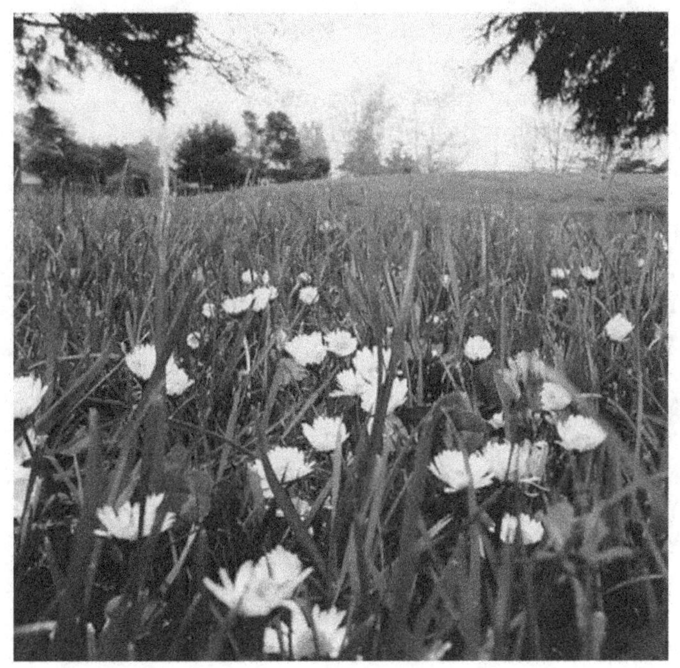

Should i give up?

Flooded with bad ideas.
Wanting to end it all.
Kill off the only mistake in mind.
Kill the one you don't truly love,
Kill yourself that's all.

Hurt yourself to feel something better than this,
You can't say sorry for not asking.
You know you don't truly matter,
You don't truly matter at all.

My hands are shaking,
My heart is breaking,
My breath should be stopping.
You know what to do,
You can end it here.
You just don't belong.

Wrists are bleeding
and you did no wrong.
Silence is your favorite song.
Reputation on the floor,
Disappointing everyone still.
You failed once more.

I do the wrong thing every time,
I guess I never learn what's right.
I can't say sorry this time,
That just won't work.
Bleed, Bleed, Bleed
Give up.
Bleed, Bleed, Bleed,
Give up.

Stop please,
My mind is killing me.
I can't be me,
I should have never drunk from the bottle.
Stop please,
My heart is breaking inside.
I should have never been alive.

All the thoughts are coming back,
All of them haunt my head.
I'm alone in my masterpiece.

10.16.19

I want to end it all,
so that I can lay on the clouds.
I want to end it all,
so people don't bother me like they do.
I want to end it now
because sadness is a one-way street.
I want to end it all
because I feel so alone.
I want to end it all because
it's just better that way if I wasn't here.
I want to end it so that I can have wings to fly to a
happier place than this mentality
I hold onto.
I want to end it all
because they don't hear me and
I don't speak loud enough.
I want to end it so this can just be over.

scars

I didn't see the harm,
I didn't see the scar.
I just wanted to get better,
I just didn't know any better.
I know you look to me,
I am ashamed for loving
you with my thorns.
I didn't accept your help,
I just thought it would be easier alone.
I didn't know that scars stayed forever.

I thought they would go away,
I thought you would stay away.
You seemed to love me more when I hurt like this.
You seemed to hear my voice lost in the sound of death.
You grabbed me by the hand and pulled me to the other side,
I didn't know scars stayed in our eyes.

I wanted to go
but I felt I shouldn't let go.
I crawled out of a pit of silence
and you were there.
You held your hand out to me,
I didn't know I was buried
in the dark of the thoughts, I had created.
I didn't know scars stayed in our eyes forever.

Blue People

Human hearts of cold steel dropped to the kitchen floor,
You had chosen more.
If we had another life you would have done nothing differently,
You say that you know you can't change.
Why do you give in to this blue neighborhood?

Human brains made of orange peel drop to the kitchen floor,
You had chosen more.
if you had a chance to do it again,
You wouldn't do it because it hurt too much before.
Why do you give in to this blue neighborhood?

The talk of blue lights,
Then blue people disappeared at once.
Your warm hearts have healed.
you can now go to the land of forever
Why did those blue people give into the neighborhood?

Broken People

I may think too much,
I have a scatter plot of a brain.
Holding on for life's awakening,
so I can see the brightest star.
Broken, hurting, holding on to faith.
I just can't see how you can love a broken person like me.
I am nothing like the sky above,
I am what you called love.
You were so good to me,
I want to see you live freely.
I will always be true for you,
You have always told me the truth.
How can someone like you love a broken person like me?
I just don't understand what I have to offer up
because you have given me so much.
You have left so much beauty in every flower you seeded,
all left here with me.
I feel so lost without you
but I never would have found me if I never found you.
I know I am broken....but I wouldn't change me
because I know you loved the broken parts of me.

Interlude .
Carry On

People walk along the old sidewalks.
Their experience has been different on that sidewalk.
They all just carry on with their daily life.
No matter what the issue.
Quick, they run home.
They scatter like birds.
They break like the ground cracks.
as always, I thought of them,
but they just carry on.

this is better

I know I have a purpose now,
I am to live.
At this moment I feel happiness
cause I have peace within myself...
Peace within my life.
I went through all this bad to get to some good.
I know there is a light at the end of my tunnel.

Chapter Thirty-Three
Memories Made

Avenue
Rose Garden
Falling Leaves
The Best
Follow Through
Years
Record Of Gold
Wow

Live in your mind, with the memories you keep safe.

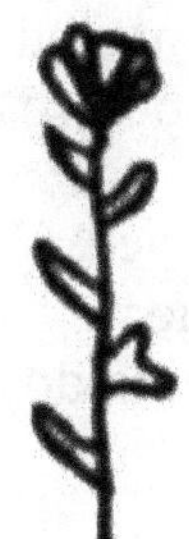

Avenue

I didn't know your reputation;
and I've been on this road before.
The way the avenue damaged me,
The way you loved me before...
It drove me crazy.
That's the love I want back.
I just need to feel you near.
I don't know what I would do if you
crushed me.
The entity you are,
Heart of gold and eyes like the ocean...
Don't break my heart,
I need you to be here.
It's the avenue
I know it hurts to stay.

Rose Garden

We walk in this place called heaven.
You seem to think I am falling out of love
but in truth, I'm not.
You just can't recognize me.
Why do the roses block the sunlight?

You wouldn't want to love
a wilting sunflower.
Take me away from this rose garden
into the fields where we can run.
Take me away to a place where
I am no longer lost,
Where I can fill your heart with seeds of love.
Can you take me out of this rose garden?

I promise to love you and your imperfections.
Take me out of this rose garden with you.
The sun is so bright on my face,
Just take me to a place where you can see me clearer too.
I just want to be with you,
I want you to remember me.

Falling Leaves

These falling leaves,
They remind me
of how I used to be.
Crunching them with my feet,
Laying in the grass,
Feeling content...
Falling leaves bring memories.
Falling leaves bring the autumn back to me.
I may not be happy now
but I was then.
These falling leaves are gracefully falling,
They fall to give me joy and hope.
These falling leaves give me
a sense of happiness.

The Best

The reality of it all is so sad.
I have parts they hurt by
people who give me issues,
that take all my tissues.
The best always burns my throat,
Like when my fingers used to feel so cold while
playing my sad song.
What a sad time it used to be,
the issue must have always been me.
The best was always good to me,
The good was always pure to see,
The purity of it all was a sad memory.

Follow Through

You can't be mad at her because she's not you and
never will be able to do all the wonderful things you
always do to come through.
You're not her and she's not you...
She's not you and you're not her.
I know you hope she gets better
but in this weather, she will never.
She's not you and you're just not her.

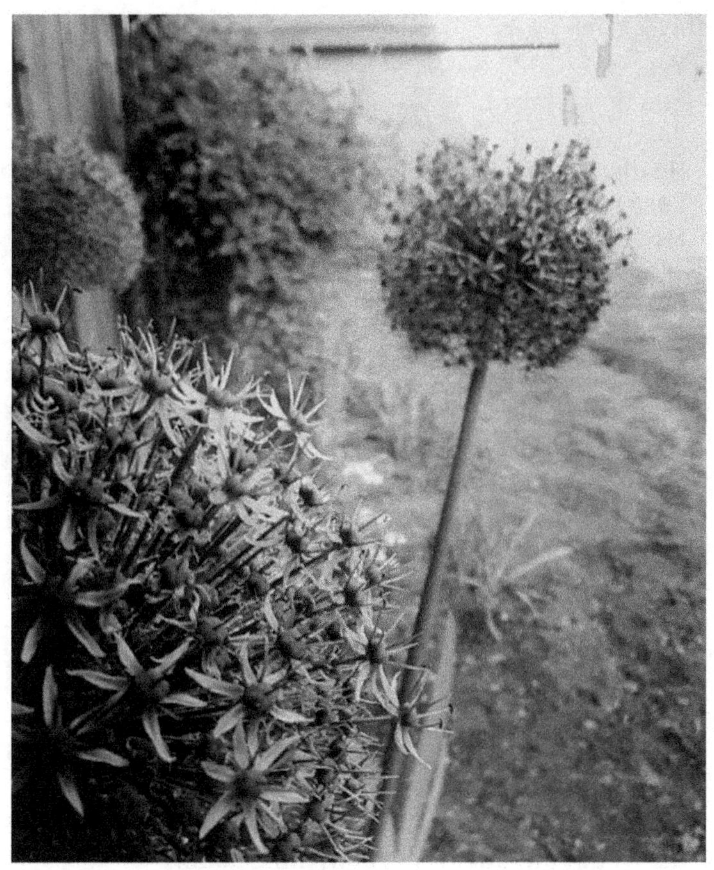

Years

Year one,
You both stayed.
Year five,
He disappeared.
Year ten,
My life came crashing down.

I was held down
but there was no ground
to hold me still.
There were only promises built on lies,
It was so tragic to see you both fall twice.
I wanted you to be here,
You were never really here.
I wanted to be held up.
I wanted you to hold my nervous hand.
I know now that I wasn't like them,
I was just the first
and the worst
you could ever have.

I know that I caused you trouble.
I lied and cheated my way through it all,
it's what you taught me if anything at all.
I swore to myself
I wouldn't end up like you two.
I wouldn't hit rock bottom
and float away like him.
I wouldn't give up
and hurt like her.

I knew that I could be better,
To become the new chapter.
The new life
that they wished they had.
I know that the beginning is the worst,
The end is when I succeed.
I needed permanent love,
someone to hold my nervous hand.

I know he's not here on my birthdays,
and she never knew how I really felt.
You knew, "fine" was never an answer
and he knows that I have been waiting for a call.

I wanted you both so much.
I cried for you,
I looked for you.
You were supposed to help me,
Help me through it all
but I handled all of the war.

I ended up with cuts and bruises.
I ended up giving up on you.
I know that forgiveness is what I must do.
I forgive you for not holding my hand,
I know it's not easy to love me.
I have said it before:

"I know I owe you the world,
but you owe me the universe"

I still love you both,
now I must lie down
and rest my head.
Year 15 of my life.
He still doesn't exist,
He just can't keep a promise.
She still looks for love,
when it's right here.
Years that I remember washed away year by year.

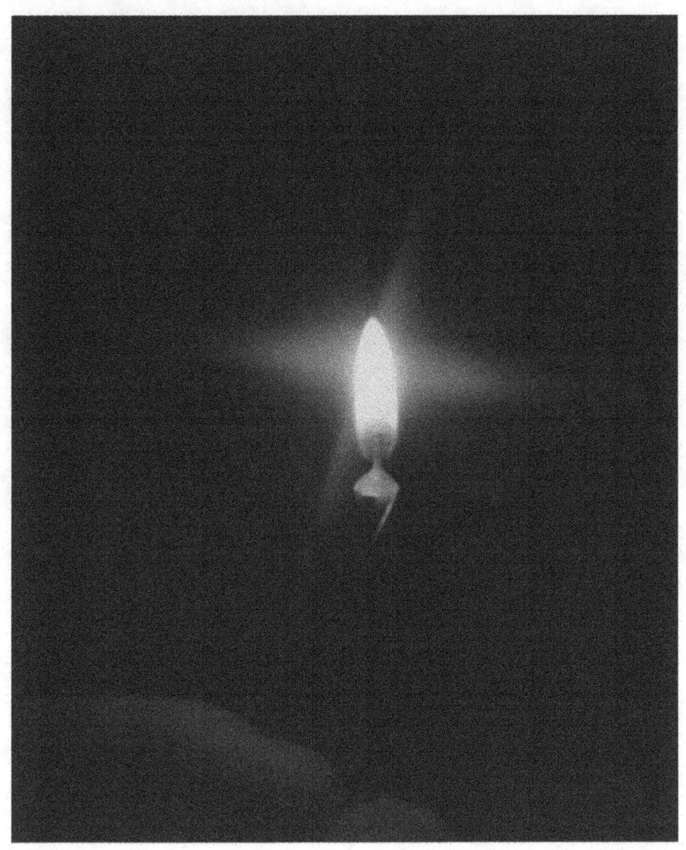

Record of gold

The record plays her story.
Her story of pain
but she made it glorious.
She made battles seem easy.
She had a record of gold,
A heart of steel,
and a hold like gravity.
She was so kind to me.
She prayed that everything
would get better for me.
Her gold record kept me going on repeat.

Wow

I remember those times,
The ones were I felt so alive
but they don't see me anymore.
I don't care like I used too.
I don't feel like I used too.
See them watching me now,
Feel the silence of the crowd.
Nobody wants to take me down,
but I don't want to have a crown.
but **wow**
see them stare,
Making me feel so dead on the outside.
Never put myself out there,
because of their cruel words,
because of hate that buried my soul.
and nobody wants to take me down,
but I don't want to have a crown.
but **wow**
look how far I have gotten
on my own.
Wow,
but *why do I feel so alone?*
Why do I,
Why do I feel so dead inside?
because I don't care like I used too,
and I don't feel like I used too.
but **wow**,
look how far I've gotten,
On. My. Own.

Chapter Thirty-Four
Soul, Blood, Body, and Past

Past is soul.
soul is body.
Body is blood.

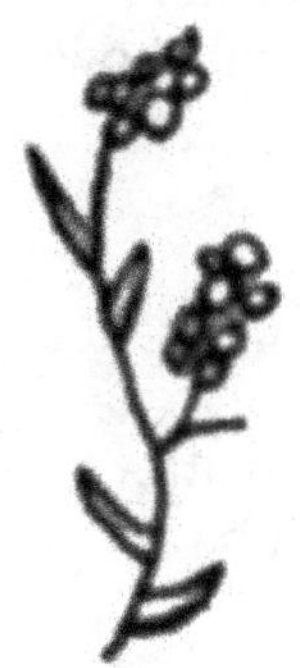

handprints

handprints are like lost love,
They can be found anywhere.
My handprint is on a soul above.
I love,
I give,
These handprints.
handprints are soul,
Are love,
Are beauty and lost in truth.
These handprints can't be
tracked through the time. . .
They are souls who left,
souls who left handprints to find.

Call me by Name

I looked for pure people,
I heard it can be found in the water.
I want to be found
and be called by name.
I believe that you were made for me.
You carry my heart
in the bucket to the dark,
Rinse my heart out in the water.
Find me in the Firefly valley
and call me by name.
I heard you loved the broken.
I heard you need new.
I want to be found
and called by name.
I feel the sunshine float away,
You can feel the darkest waves
in the sea of the drama.
I want to be found
and called by name.
Call me by name
and I will take you to the river,
where we will float away
to the pure.

careful fingers

I am loved.
I am happy
I am laughing.
I worked with my careful fingers
to build the house.
I created with blood, sweat, and tears.
I run my careful fingers across
the wooden table to find the truth.
I made the ones I love so proud.
I hope you see that now.
I built all that I have with
these careful fingers.
I can rest them now.

Breaking the Known

Moving on seems so easy.
I know that I have the energy to push through.
I can be the masterpiece I see.
I can see the daylight of me.
I am the one with the known
but it's time to break the known.
I know that I trace in circles but this time
I will go in a different direction.
Moving on seemed so easy
but I can't let go of the known.

I follow the road to the truest love.
Moving on seemed so easy
but I know I will come back.
Breaking the known isn't easy.
I just have to let go.
I will push the block of the known to the unknown
where I can breathe, finally for me.

Blankets

Can you cover me?
Can you keep me from the cold?
Can you be beside me?
Can I have you there to hold?
Can I love you?
Can I lay by you?
Will you cover me when I'm cold?
When I'm scared?
When I don't know who I am?
Will you be there?
Will you cover me with blankets?
Block all the darkness?
Will you?
Will you care when I don't?
Will you give when I won't?
Will you tell me when I'm wrong?
Please say you will
because I need someone to cover me
when I'm cold,
When I'm alone,
When I don't know you anymore.
Will you be there?
Will you cover me with blankets?
Block all the darkness?
Will you?
Say you will.
Please, don't leave me alone.
Please, will you cover me?
When I'm cold?

Glitter

feeling the glitter fall out my eyes when I cry about
losing you for the first time.

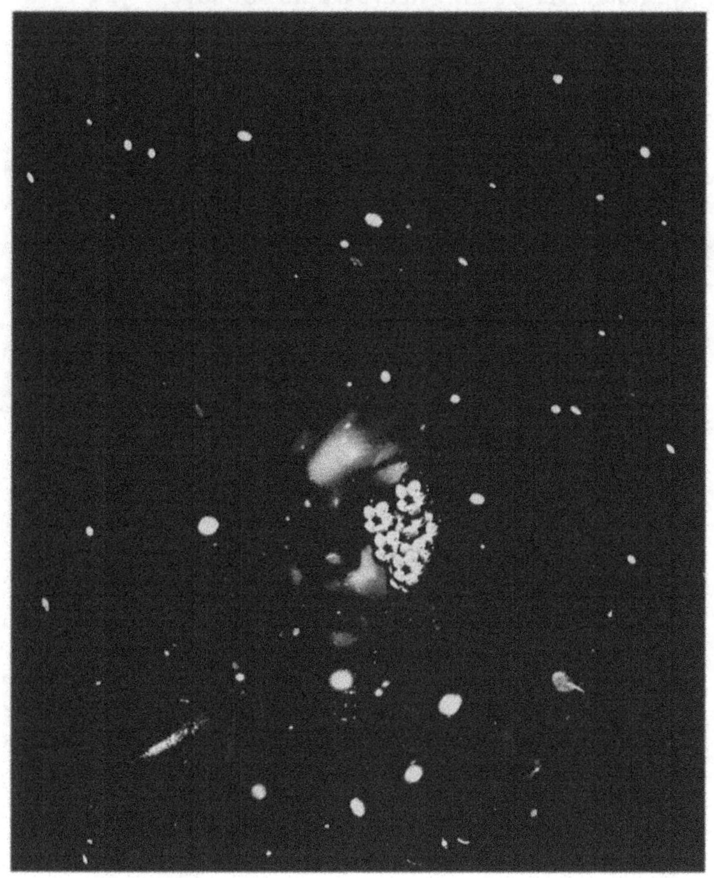

Where is my love?

If I had given you my soul would you love
me more?
If I had given you my heart would you love
me more?
If I had given you my body would you love
me more?
If I had given you my blood would you love me more?
Where is my love even now that you have all of me?
Where are you hiding it?
Where can I find it?
Where is my love?

safety first

Replace the scars with Band-Aids,
Tie up the laces of your shoes,
You have to have safety first.
I know that you and I only fight,
That's why I can't stay.
Broken is what you called me
and I never felt so thin.
I never knew even your words could be cruel when
they used to love me.
Tightened the ropes for my walk,
I look both ways,
Safety always comes first.
I feel your pain and I am sorry.
I know that going wasn't your plan but I can't sit in
the toxicity of your mind.
Your words bring my clouds down.
Your heart has fallen asleep,
so to keep me safe...go back.
I know safety always comes first
with me and my heart.

Goodbye, Lover

Taking time to burn the pictures,
Taking time to read the chapters.
I wasn't going to leave
but you won't,
so I have to get out of this
apartment of failed dreams.
I think I am going back to Montana
where I can think freely.
I didn't want to go and leave you like this
but you gave me no choice.
I had to keep my heart and soul safe
from the rage.
I will write to you
to make sure you're okay.
I love you, Lover, this is goodbye.

Moments I Live

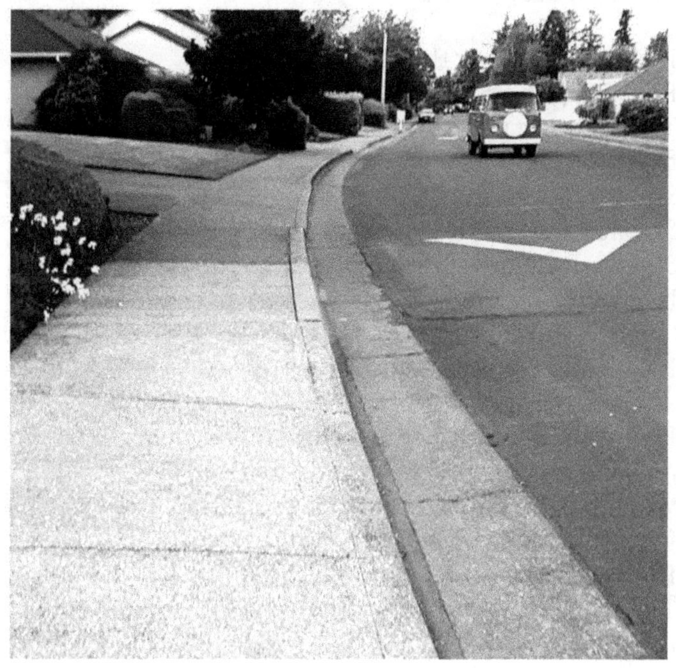

the cathedral

I walk the halls of the cathedral,
Revisiting the past.
The painting paints the pain beautifully and I revisit
that memory.
She was a girl and I was a boy.
She had flaws and I had none in her eyes.
She wanted more but I didn't have the card
in my hand.
So she went out to find a man.
I was left brokenhearted
and she left where we started.
I went through all her ups and downs
and she just sat there with a frown
when I asked for the best of her.
I walk the halls of the cathedral,
Revisiting the past.
The painting paints the pain beautifully and I revisit
the memory.
I was young and she was not.
She had hurt and I was lost.
I had fear and she had lost so much,
I couldn't reach her fast enough.

I walk the halls of the cathedral,
Revisiting the past.
The painting paints the pain beautifully and I revisit the memory.
I was finally locked up.
I had no freedom.
I had no idea that I was a bad guy.
She painted me a villain in her eyes.
Her eyes don't see quite right.
I went mad in my cage,
I finally let go of the past.
I walk the halls of the cathedral,
Revisiting the past.
The painting paints the pain beautifully and I revisit the memory.

Interlude . Breaking, Falling, Repeating

I know more now that I have fallen,
I feel more now that I broke,
I see more now that I repeat love.
I move on so that you can too.
I leave so you can get up and go.
I break, fall, and repeat. . .

IV

Now my petals are wilted,
I know that it was all of me now.
It was all my fault for staying
or wanting to stay. . .
I see this now and I have to just shut her out.
It's good for both of us.
I will be happy. . .
You may be happy
but I can only speak for myself.
I may not know what you went through after me but
I know that I am not done growing tall.

Chapter Thirty-Five
Small

Intro - Error
Recess
Run
Splinters
Pluto
Drown
Scarecrow

How can you feel lost and beautiful at the same time?

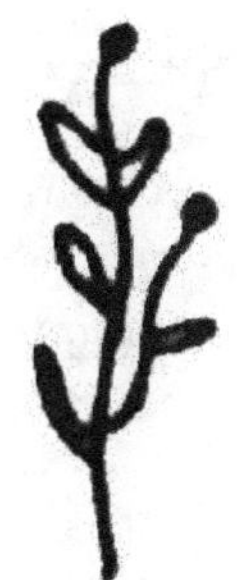

Error

You see me as a friend.
I see you as nothing
but an error, in my system.
You lied,
You cheated.
How am I supposed to live
on knowing you did these things?
I trusted you
and you hurt me.
Instead of loving me.
All you said was "okay"
and left me with nothing at all
but your errors.

Recess

This is no reset,
No playtime.
I need to decompress
from all the bad times.
I needed a recess,
I need a break from you.
It's okay I can leave you.

Run

You always run away in fear.
You always leave me in tears.
I won't solve all your problems,
You have to fix them yourself.
I don't hate you
but you always run away from me.
Am I a waste of life in your eyes?
I am sorry for being honest with you.
I am well aware that I hurt you,
when I stopped running with you.
You don't love me anymore,
You can keep running in fear.
At least I know now,
it wasn't me who was falling apart.

Splinters

Different feel when you walk in the room,
I hear you talking about how much
you miss him.
I can hear your heartbeat,
it is going in a different direction.
I can feel that distance when you're here,
I know you miss him.
I can almost hear him laugh in the distance.
Each time a splinter
is what I get in return
for loving you.
Everyone but me sees
that you want him more,
Why am I not enough?

Pluto

Cold and scared,
I wish you would know who I was.
I am no longer me
because of your changes.
Am I a planet or a dwarf?
Am I just a rock in space?
I don't want to know who I am anymore.
Gravity is always pulling me,
I go from side to side, in this space.
Only you make the rules,
If you could know how I felt
maybe you would change the rules?
If you only knew how I feel right now.
I don't want to be this rock anymore.

Drown

I woke up in a case of dark water,
Saw the roses floating above my pale skin.
Felt the dirty hands of angels hold me down;
Swimming has never been easy for me.
Let me drown now,
as their scary-red faces fade away.
Going insane sometimes felt so good.
I screamed for the water to go out through that small
drain, in the bottom,
at the bottom of the cold case to escape.
Felt the ocean waves crash against my face.
I know I can't fight it anymore.

Scarecrow

Pick on me you old crows,
I won't fall from my post.
Take my corn
and fly away.

Fill me with straw, my old friend.
Take me down,
Before it's too late.
The children are killers
with flames.
Tell them that the Angel is dead.

Scarecrow, Scarecrow, where are you?

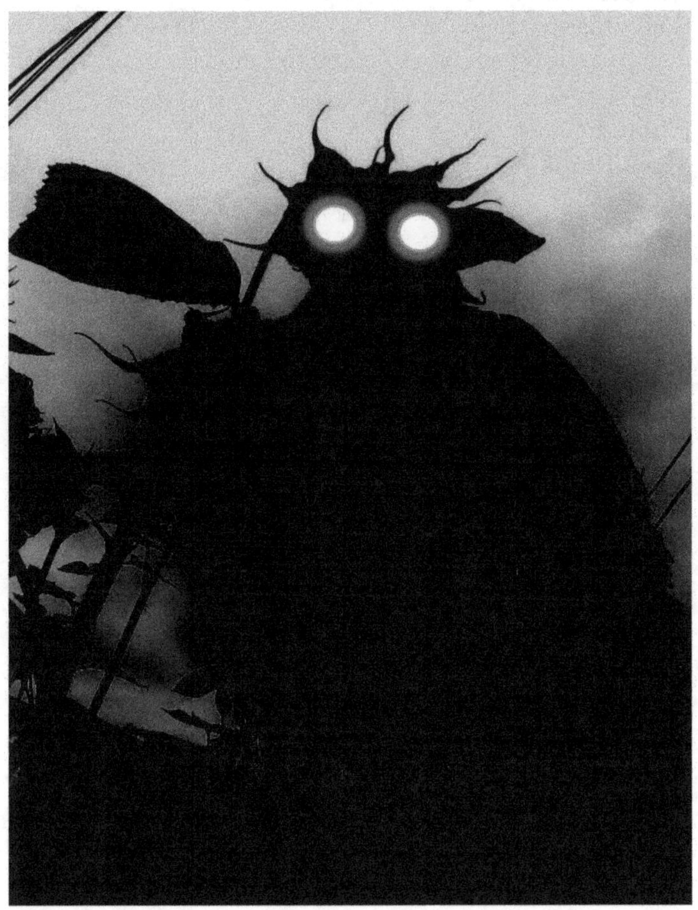

Chapter Thirty-Six
Too Close To Say

Too
Thought
Light Bulbs
Close
Laugh and Die
To
Wish Me Well
City Lights
Say
Decaying
Up
The one-winged canary

One of the hardest things to do in my life is letting go of what I thought was true.

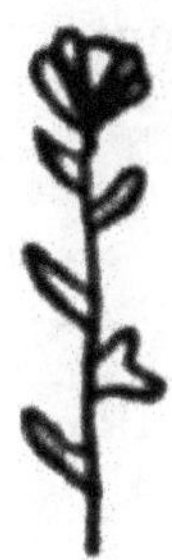

Too

Too many mistakes for trying again.
Only if I didn't try so hard,
Only if I could retry again.

Thought

I always thought about me.
I never had trust in us,
I had to lookout
for what you might do.
I always thought it could work.
I never knew I could love.
I always thought I was broken.
I never knew. . .

Light bulbs

You glow with visible light,
You bring electric heat with every move.
You shine in every room
but you get jealous.
I see that now.
You let the darkness take over;
You don't even fight it.
Why can't you be like Light bulbs?
The others here are not demanding.
They understand me and you do not.
You say I'm good for you;
I doubt that is true.
These statements
are too close to say the words I have to
but believe me when I say *love.*
You keep pushing me over the edge.
I guess when you burn out.
You will take my light for yourself.
so that's why I can't show my light anymore.
The light is here
but not from you.
There are other light bulbs with light for you;
I'm just not one of them for you.

Close

Cry for me when I go,
Let me go, when I reach the end.
Open up a bottle and sigh.
Stick to the old ways.
Even if I really didn't matter to you.

laugh & die

if you laugh and die.
you will be happy.
if you laugh and die.
you might be sad.
if you laugh and die.
if you laugh and die.
you may cry.
if you laugh and die.
you may never see again.
if you laugh and die.
you may never breathe again
and if you laugh and die.
youll never say goodbye.
so if you laugh and die...

To

Take me away,
Old roads always end though.

Wish Me Well

Will you wish me well?
When I'm sad?
When I'm gone?
When I need your love?
When I need you here?
Will you wish me well?
Will you?
because I want you to.
Will you?
because I need you too.
Just wish me well.
Will you pray for me?
Will you give all your love?
Even when I'm not me?
When I'm sick?
Will you
wish me well?
I know... I know, you will

City Lights

I can't forget your City lights.
I seem to remember all of them.
I can't forget
how bright they were.
You were my brother.
You were my light.
The one I could find.
so easily it was taken
and I am so sorry
but love is all I could give you.
I wonder how someone can create
such a brilliant person,
How you came to be a great friend.
How your lights shine from the sky
and of the below
but I just love those City lights.

Say

Stay and I will make you happy.
All you want is here but
you want the world.

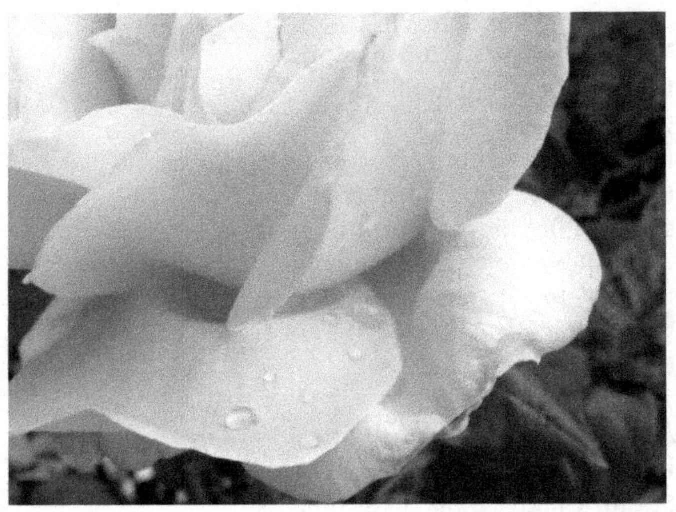

Decaying

I have been breaking down,
Not getting out of town,
Leaving my joy on the ground...
I have been decaying.
It wasn't good for me.
I left it on the floor,
I don't know myself anymore
but I am not looking for it no more
I have been decaying inside.
I left my love to the side.
I haven't left the house in a few days.
Maybe I am in a place
where I can't leave.
A place where I can't be me.
Where I am decaying and not free...
but now I have a place for me.
Peace of mind to the harsh reality.
The thing I see through my eyes,
The place where I can find the time to be the one that I am,
The being of mind and hope...
so I am gonna be decaying for a while;
Decaying inside of my mind.

Left the light at the end of the road.
I never gave someone the best of me
or the true story of my Life:
The decaying side of me.
Decaying is where I lay.
I feel that way from time to time.
I am decaying inside of my skin.
My blood has stopped flowing through my veins
but I will be fine with it for a while,
Until I'm in that box
with flowers every year, like an anniversary
of my same decaying sadness inside.
I will just die in that side of my mind.
I will decay inside my soul,
Then die and be free from it all.

Up

Blank faces, Pretty cases.
Black umbrellas and you.
Sitting under gravel.
Do I know which direction to take?
I hope for you above to find love, somehow.
Down here the Angel says Up, Up, Up.
Down here the Demons say Down, Down, Down.
and I say No, No, No.
I don't think I'm ready now?

White stars, Pretty scars.
With or without, I'm lost in a picture frame.
Lying beneath the grass now.
Which way should I go?
I hope my picture burns, someday.
Down here it feels like nothing.
There are things that I didn't know until now.
That the Angel says Up, Up
That the Demons say Down, Down.
and I say No, No.
No, I'm not ready now.

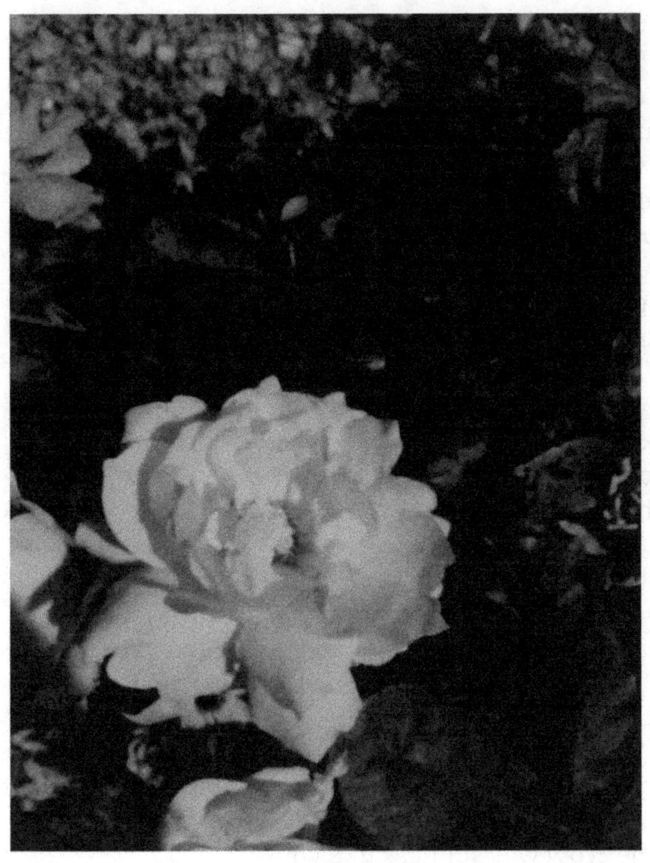

The one-winged canary

My pain on your wall like the art in the sky,
Shadows overflow when I close one eye.
Your biggest regret should be the lie,
In the end, I was just the victim every time.
I wish I could have told the yellow child
to stay high
and not dwell in the cage of blue.

Sunflowers wilted beneath the cage.
Life in a still for the sun has no light for me.
The cage is the safest place I know because
everything else was evil in your eyes
of knowing.
for you, I tried and tried but when you're broken on
the outside as well as the inside,
I couldn't help you escape.
She had clipped my wing and told me that I was
bad.....I was just trying to live my truth.
I am a one-winged canary but I still love the earth.

Kept quiet so no one could hear my song of truth,
The lines you gave were false.
I trusted a crow in the luck to survive your wasteland
of a domain.
The crow was soulless like you.
Oh, say the truth sets us all free but my truth would
kill me.
I am a one-winged canary but I still love the earth.

You may have seen the brokenness of my heartache
in pain but you still stood there and watched my
peace unravel.
The smell of new is as fresh as the lavender in
Grandma's backyard.
You have a black heart-shaped into the light she saw
to protect your truest form...
you are evil.
I am a one-winged canary but I still love the earth.

The years I sailed on the river of not knowing
whether to give in or fake it was the peace and quiet I
never knew I needed.
I had bowed to you in tears for mercy but, of course,
loving the devil was the key to your heart.
The years I sat in the rusted cage when I could have
flown outside to discover my heart and art but I sat in
the cage wondering why I was even here at all.
I am a one-winged canary but I still love the earth.

I was the magic in the air but it was all locked away,
so you could be the stars.
My universe sacrificed because I loved you and
wanted you to be happy even though my wing was
cut and I was locked
in a cage of blue.
I am a one-winged canary but I still love the earth.

I'm sorry for being the trouble of your life,
so cry for I have taken the only real love ever received.
I am going to fly not by wings but by my belief to rise from this ash you made
in my cage of blue.
The copper keys left on the tree where you left me to perish,
I will unlock the cage of blue at last.
I will fly like the earth wrote for me.
My blood is pouring into the earth so your black heart can pump clean.
My wings damaged by your words of poison but my heart is all I need to love the brokenness of the world.
I may be a one-winged canary but I still love the earth.

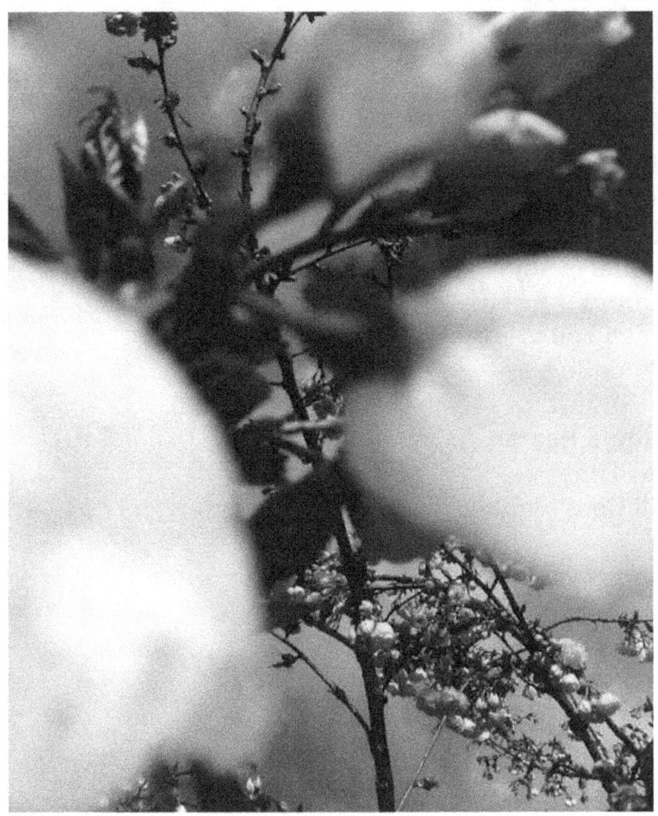

Chapter Thirty-Seven
The End

Nothing but Heart
HEADSPACE
My Cloud
for Me
Broken Floorboards
Home is Anywhere
Empty
Love You
Blooming
PUREVOC
Liquid Heart
No Time
All Goes Blank

Don't ever put your hope in someone's eyes
cause some people don't change.

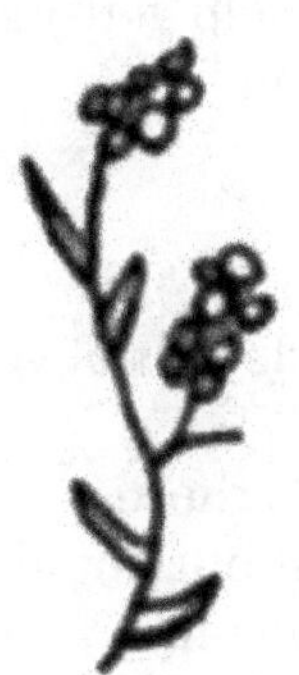

Nothing but heart

I did everything I could do to save you
but you did not want help getting up.
I miss you now that you fell.
You fell for him,
He broke your heart.
I am nothing but heart,
I even wear it on my sleeves of yellow.
I want you to know
that I would have been there.
You still say I am great but not great enough.
That's okay I will move on.

HEADSPACE

Don't let them RENT it out,
and pull YOU down.
They don't deserve your TIME.
You can SCREAM out loud,
and tell them what you're ALL about.
and if you won't give them HEADSPACE,
They can't TAKE advantage of you.
Give them nothing less but the pretty picture of YOU.

My Cloud

Lift me up,
Take me down.
I know it will never rain,
in my desert.
I will sit on my cloud
and watch the chaos form.
In my cloud, I will have love.
In my cloud, I wish to have happiness within.
In my cloud, I will live as nothing has changed.
In my cloud, I will truly be happy.

for Me

Let me take you to my happy place,
Just you and I.
Just imagine us in my lavender fields,
Living is easy with peace and joy.
It doesn't matter much to me if you want to leave,
This is for me.
Nothing to be mad about,
It may be crazy to say I would rather
be here alone.
It will always be alright to leave.
Let me take you to my lavender fields.
Always know that things could be dreams,
You and I could be my slumber but
let me just walk down
to my lavender fields for the last time.

Broken Floorboards

You had a drinking problem,
I told you I would be here.
You said I just didn't care,
I do care but I won't watch you die.
I want to love you
but you walk on broken Floorboards.
The holes are just too deep,
I may bleed when I walk with you.
Loving you may have a side effect.
I want to love but I am scared,
I don't want to be the one in the danger zone.
Loving you was always goodbye.

Home is Anywhere

Take my hand,
Look into my hazel eyes.
I can take you home,
Home is anywhere you want it to be.
I know you may get scared,
I promise I won't let you get hurt.
I will comfort you along the way,
I think we can make it out there.
Home can be anywhere as long as I have you.
if you need me I will be here,
as long as I can call you home.

Empty

Our love was always on fire
but after you left I felt so empty.
I know you miss me,
You told me in the letter you sent.
When I lost you it was like I lost balance.
I feel more empty than when I loved you.
I truly feel like I need you now,
We were a match made in our suffering.
We were fiction.
I feel more empty than when I loved you.
I wonder what happened to us,
I truly wonder why I feel this way.
I'm left empty filled with that distance you made.

Love you

I admit I am greedy,
I just want your affection.
Say love you and go.
You already know I want to dance in the fire,
I want to pour the oil under our romance.
I come back to life when I feel your love.
I admit I miss you every moment,
I don't ever want to misplace you.
Just say love you and go.
Just say....go away.

Blooming

As a kid, I always sat in the background,
I never found out what real friends were
until the fifth grade.
I never thought I would grow up,
now I don't think I want to.
In the end, I thought it would be lovely
but now I only see the darkness.
All you ever said was goodbye.
I never thought that the day would come.
I never knew I could bloom without you.
I never knew I would grow up,
I never knew I would pass the darkness
but I guess I knew that I
would grow like a tall sunflower,
I would Bloom at the finest hour.
All I know is that I loved all of you.
At least I know my end.

PUREVOC

Help me, I'm all alone,
I can't lose myself.
I think I outran my shadow.
I wish I was the one that everybody wanted.
They want the mask and that is okay,
if they wish for that.
I can hideaway for a few more years.
The ones who cover up beware, I'm there too.

Liquid Heart

I am getting weak,
My hair is gray.
My face has wrinkles,
From all those years.
The years I spent Wondering,
Why do we grow old?
I just want to live with the ones I love,
Be there for them when they don't understand.
My heart has turned to liquid.
My mind doesn't remember all the facts anymore,
My legs don't walk the same.
My ears hear things at night,
My eyes see differently than before.
I want my lover to know I loved them,
I want to be there for them
when their feeling so blue.
My heart has now turned to liquid
and my life is turning its final page.

No time

I have no time to waste.
I have no time left,
I need you to know I am done.
I have no time for lies.
No time for you.
I made an excuse for me to use:
I know I don't have long before
my eyes close forever.

All goes blank

I saw your face, in the end.
I remember when you left,
I swear I didn't expect to fall.
I could just lay here and die
but *what will it do for me?*
When all went blank,
I never thought that I would escape.
I struggle in this cage of nothingness.
I rise up and fall again.
I could just lay here and die
but I need to just breathe.
I saw your eyes and I felt nothing.
I could have just laid there and died,
but *what would it do for me?*
I would lose my lavender fields,
I would lose my cloud,
I would even lose you.
At this point, the struggle for love is lost,
I can love me more than anything
to erase all the dark.
I take my last love breath here.

thank you. creator. for giving me life to
live. now i have made it to the other
side. . .
i see the clearest blues in the sky.
i see the brightest yellows of all the
planets combined.
i see the darkest reds within the past
and i let it go for myself to finally be
free. i unlocked the cage at last and i
know now how to be happy. . .
i know how to be human

sincerely bultman

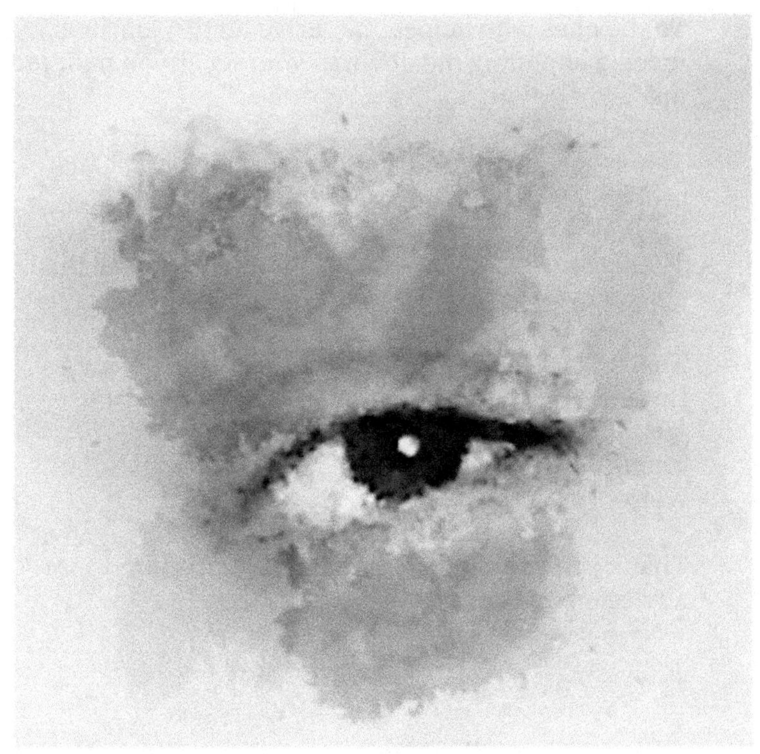

Thank you's

To the ones who helped me thrive on this journey instead of pulling me down to your level, you built me up.

Thank you, Kendall, for taking amazing photos that took the emotion of the poetry to another level.

Thank you, Jill, for the marvelous advice and all the support you gave.

Thank you, Unpredictable Four, for being the best three friends I could have ever asked for.

Thank you, to my family, for being supportive of this work of art.

Thank you to anyone else that has contributed some advice or support of any kind.

Author's note

"Moments I Live" has been one of the many things I kept for myself, for the last four years. Now it is finally the worlds, I want to say that by any means this work was not meant to offend or hurt anyone's feelings. This work is meant to be here for you when you need to feel seen. "Moments I Live" is a journey of life in all its worst and best moments.

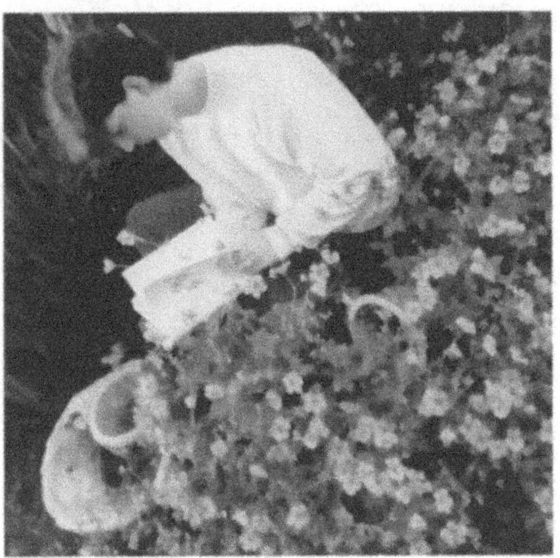

If you have any questions just email or message using one of the following:

Instagram: @bultman717

Email: Bultman717@gmail.com

Website: Bultmanshop.com

www.ingramcontent.com/pod-product-compliance
Lightning Source LLC
LaVergne TN
LVHW012337100826
845148LV00018B/2702

9780578699660